PRAISE FOR THE AUTHOR

"Among the ranks of Greta Thunberg and the students of Parkland High School, Jett James Pruitt is a powerful force in the movement of young people shaping our country's future. His rare voice of *progressive conservatism* is a refreshing change from the far-left radical ideology of his generation, and bridges the gap between conservative values and economic equality the majority of Americans have long been waiting for."

—*BooksOnPolitics.com*

"I've been privileged to know Jett since he was a young child. I became particularly aware of his keen interest in presidential politics and gifted him with my life's collection of political memorabilia. Today, he is a compelling voice of young America and his first book, *Through the Eyes of a Young American,* is vital for our future and important for us all to read."

—*Rev. Dr. C. William Mercer*
Author, Activist, and Spiritual Leader

"When my son was almost three years old, his Autism doctor told me to cancel my college savings plan because my child would probably never speak, let alone write or attend mainstream schools. Well, the book you are about to read was written by *that* child. And may his incredible words of unity, strength, and common-sense tear down every invisible wall dividing this country with the power of a thousand armies."

—*Mylo Carbia, "The Queen of Horror"*
Bestselling Author and Hollywood Screenwriter

THROUGH
THE EYES
of a
YOUNG
AMERICAN

A Teenager's Perspective on
Government, Politics and Solving
Our Country's Biggest Problems

JETT JAMES PRUITT

VANDERBILT
PUBLISHING

VANDERBILT
PUBLISHING

Published in the United States of America by Vanderbilt Publishing LLC, 2000 PGA Boulevard, Suite 4440, Palm Beach Gardens, FL 33408, USA. www.VanderbiltPublishing.com

Library of Congress Cataloging-in-Publication data is available upon request.

Print ISBN 9780996565295
Kindle ISBN 9780996565271
eBook ISBN 9780996565288

Edited by Melissa Gray
Cover Design by T. Kanseristia
Interior Design by Colleen Sheehan
Author Photos by M.C. Lund
Publicity by Ellison PR

www.JettJamesPruitt.com

ABOUT THE AUTHOR

BORN MAY 25, 2005, in Palm Beach County, Florida, **Jett James Pruitt** is an award-winning speaker, student, political strategist, founder and editor-in-chief of the political blog, *TheGenZPost.com*.

Raised on the Upper East Side in New York City, Jett was diagnosed with "moderate to severe autism" at the age of two and was completely non-verbal until the age of four. After numerous early-intervention programs and holistic treatments, Jett shocked the medical community with his recovery and formally lost his Autism diagnosis by the age of six.

Jett's unique interest in politics began at the age of nine, blossoming with the 2016 presidential election. His very first book, *Through The Eyes Of A Young American*, was written when Jett was fourteen years old and attending the eighth grade.

Today, Jett enjoys living with his mother and stepfather in Palm Beach, Florida. He maintains excellent grades while attending school online, and looks forward to publishing more political books, attending college and law school, and ultimately working in Washington, D.C. in the areas of politics, justice, and journalism.

THROUGH
THE EYES
of a
YOUNG
AMERICAN

DEDICATION

---

*This Book is Dedicated to
My Grandmother,*

Ana "Nancy" Valentin Carbia
(April 19, 1940 - August 3, 2019)

Rest In Peace, Grandma Nancy.

TABLE OF CONTENTS

"Actually, to be an effective person politically in this country, I think you have to be thirty or over, and also you have to be rich, well-placed, you have to be close to power. And I don't think that young people, because they look young, can do much, as I think they are counterproductive."

—*Kurt Vonnegut, Author*

"What I try to tell young people is that if you come together with a mission, and it's grounded with love and a sense of community, you can make the impossible, possible."

—*Rep. John Lewis, Politician*

INTRODUCTION

The Spirit of America

AS I WRITE this, the world has shut down. Stock markets have crashed. All schools are closed. Businesses are locked. Restaurants and movie theaters are dark. Grocery store shelves are bare. Weddings, funerals, concerts, conferences, and graduations are banned. Disney World is closed. All professional sports leagues have cancelled their seasons. My spring break trip to Italy is postponed. My community pool is shut down. It's illegal for me to visit the beach across the street. I am fourteen years old, sitting in a dark bedroom at home, with no distractions a normal teenager should be avoiding while making final revisions to this book— not knowing if it will serve as *The Diary of Anne Frank* during the COVID-19 Coronavirus Pandemic of 2020, or if it will be the wake-up call politicians need to hear from America's youngest generation, as I had originally intended.

"FOURSCORE AND SEVEN years ago, our fathers brought forth on this continent, a new nation, conceived in liberty, and dedicated to the proposition that all men are created equal..."

These words, profoundly spoken by our sixteenth president nearly two hundred years ago, barely scratch the surface of how truly resilient and diverse the spirit of America is.

There is no question, America means many different things to many different people.

In the eyes of young children, America means patriotic memories at amusement parks and sporting events like Disneyland, NASCAR, and The Super Bowl. For Wall Street tycoons, America is symbolized by high-priced luxury items that only those who have conquered a capitalist system could ever afford. For average working-men, America is the hot sun of the day and the cool of night. For adolescents, it is the bustling shopping mall used as a meeting place to see their pals. For immigrants, America is the opportunity to leave poverty or the restriction of wealth accumulation behind, and the chance to change one's socioeconomic class through hard work and discipline.

America is 'the land of the free' for most individuals, with its Constitution guaranteeing fundamental human rights widely held sacred, such as the right to a free press, the freedom of speech, the right to a jury trial, the right to bear arms, and many more.

America is even known for placing its core values of liberty and opportunity above birth status—a unique characteristic many other countries do not share.

But in reality, America is much more than that.

It is the enchanting spirit that inspired Christopher Columbus—with the *Niña*, the *Pinta*, and the *Santa Maria*—to sail west in 1492 to discover a new trade route to the Indies, where he could obtain riches of pearls, gold, and spices. Like a siren singing on a rock, the spirit of America led him to its discovery, which forever forged and solidified the bridge from the Old World to the New.

America represents the pioneer spirit that gave hope to more than twelve million immigrants as they ventured across difficult gateways to the land of opportunity. America represents the confidence people vest in themselves, as hundreds of thousands of ambitious men, women, and children ventured across the drylands to strike it rich during the California Gold Rush.

But most of all, America represents the fighting spirit that allowed early colonists to break free from Mother

England in an effort to seek religious, individual, and economic freedom. A struggle that somehow garnered an unimaginable victory against the tyrannical and oppressive hands of the British Crown.

This fighting spirit even sparked change within itself to abolish the enslavement, discrimination, and exploitation of the African race; the condemnation of the belittling of women; and the establishment of marital rights within the LGBTQ community.

America is perhaps the most uniquely diverse and prosperous nation in the world. But it is also true that with all of its beauty, America has several fatal flaws, with incidents and controversies that stain the reputations of both good and bad men throughout our history, and the progress that followed its birth has not been an easy effort. In fact, it took the backs of millions of slaves; the blood, sweat, and fears of underage factory workers; the protests and pleas of men, women, and children; the brutal force of protective services; the incarceration of innocent people; the rewriting of the U.S. Constitution; and the time and energy of the most notable activists and visionaries, to take us where we are today.

From historical figures like Frederick Douglass, Sojourner Truth, Susan B. Anthony, Harriet Tubman, Elizabeth Cady Stanton, to the more recent voices of Gloria Steinem, Martin Luther King, Jr., and Ruth Bader Ginsberg, common individuals have significantly changed the way America treats its citizens legally and through character. We must never forget their efforts, nor their desire for change, for if we do, we will most certainly forget their ideals.

As we have seen so vividly with this pandemic, today's law may not be the *law of the land* forever. And what we must do as young American citizens is follow their example, replicate and quadruple their efforts, to not only preserve their change and vision, but to also apply the spirit of America itself, to resolve whatever further issues and controversies we might face in both the foreseeable and the long-term futures of this country.

We must never let our collective guard down, for there will always be conflict—a perpetual war between freedom and slavery, ignorance and knowledge, and strength and weakness. This struggle consumes us all as global citizens, not just the United States. Let our forefathers' efforts to win this ongoing war not go in vain. Let us never forget the past, but let us also never praise the previous mistakes of this country, and let us move forward to a brighter and more peaceful world.

So, it is within this context that I describe a new vision for the future of America, particularly for my generation, and for those generations before me stewarding our fate until we arrive. Given my birth year of 2005, I claim *Generation Z* as my own, and at the time of this writing, I am unsure if I am witnessing the birth of America's first corporatocracy, or if the severe economic damage caused by Coronavirus COVID-19 will change our global landscape forever, or if unknown forces in the sky will emerge as our creators and true leaders.

The truth is, I have no idea how the events of today will eventually play out, or if my opinions will radically shift when I turn forty-five years old, or if the burning issues of our time will be solved by a simple pill, device, or robot of the future.

But what I do know is that a new strand of thinking is required to move us all forward during this incredibly polarized climate of red states versus blue states, billionaires versus blue collars, and conservatives versus progressives. And with this book, I offer solutions to the most pressing issues facing our country today, knowing each chapter will be quoted by my future political opponents who will hold the words of my fourteen-year-old self against me should solid facts and indisputable evidence sway my future self to think otherwise. Still, I am confident and willing to present these ideas and allow them to be preserved forever.

It is no secret that our corporate-sponsored, two-party political system is at the root of our troubles. The constant bickering within bipartisan chambers is eroding the fabric of this country, while millions of Americans worry about affording food, rent, student loans, health insurance, and medical bills. Even those who achieve responsible, upper middle-class success know they are only one layoff, health crisis, or housing market crash away from losing their perfect FICO score and claiming bankruptcy.

To most Americans, the formerly accessible *American Dream* now appears to be a mirage, available only for those who have started a successful company or purchased a winning lottery ticket. For this reason, it is more important than ever that we abandon political partisanship, histrionic rhetoric, and identity politics. Now, more than ever, we must strive to fight the status quo, to think *inside* the box, and label ourselves as Americans first instead of making our differences our dividing lines in the sand.

Sure, this sounds familiar, but *how* do we do this?

Unlike many of the politicians currently occupying the halls of Capitol Hill, I believe progressive and conservative values are *not* mutually exclusive, can peacefully coexist, and make for a balanced, cohesive American society that will grow even stronger as we reach the next century.

The following chapters will elaborate on my vision for healthcare, taxation, social security, tariffs, trade policies, automation, climate change, education, labor issues, welfare, military spending, national security, border security, universal basic income, capitalism, entrepreneurism, abortion, gun violence, and human trafficking.

I thank you in advance for joining me on this journey.

Now, let's begin.

CHAPTER 1

Healthcare

IF I WERE to describe my entire political belief system in a single phrase, I would declare that I am "pro-human from conception to grave." I am strongly in favor of preserving life at all stages of development: from conception to birth, from childhood to adulthood, and from old age to death. I believe it is the role of government to ensure that every citizen is afforded a chance to obtain the great economic opportunities that exist within our society, which includes providing every American with affordable healthcare.

Healthcare is one of the most heated political issues in the United States. What many do not realize is that a solid healthcare system is key for keeping peace within our society, as well as the preservation of individual health. Imagine how quickly our government would shatter if a second black plague infected the majority of our citizens? Hospitals would shut down. Martial law would have to be enacted. Our social contract would be voided. Therefore, an affordable, effective, and accessible system built to encourage the *prevention of illness* benefits society as a whole, not just an individual and their loved ones.

Many people on the left side of the political spectrum believe healthcare is an essential government service and feel that all American citizens should be guaranteed access to affordable treatments. They argue the United States should implement a single-payer healthcare system, which is when the costs of medical services are funded by a single money pool of taxpayer dollars. This would cover every resident via one single payer system, much like the current system for military veterans who are covered one hundred percent by the VA hospital system.

According to the United States Census Bureau, *Healthcare Insurance Coverage in the United States: 2017*, About 28.5 million people in our country go without health insurance, which equates to 8.8 percent of the population of the United States being uninsured. And according to the Organization for Economic Cooperation and Development (OECD) in *Health at a Glance in 2017: OECD Indicators*, the United States was one of only six countries out of the 36 members of the group that has not implemented a universal health care system.

As a teenager, not only do I vehemently support the idea of a universal right to health care for all American citizens, it's also very hard for me to understand why we did not implement a single-payer system years ago, particularly during the recovery following The Great Depression.

It is easy for anyone to point out that as a young man who has never had a job, or the need to pay taxes or medical bills, that a proper understanding of the complex economic issues behind healthcare may evade me. Still, it is hard to comprehend how the most prosperous nation in the world was outdone by countries like Australia, Canada, England, Spain, Italy, Finland, Germany, Ireland, Israel, Sweden, Norway, and Portugal, who somehow all figured out how to pay for universal healthcare, while we still have not.

Our government's duty to provide guaranteed quality healthcare is second only to its duty to provide national security. It is undoubtedly the most important social service any government can provide. Moreover, I have studied the economics behind various single-payer proposals and believe the United States will actually spend *less* money on healthcare if we guarantee the right to it. Public health will improve. Medical bankruptcies will disappear. Small businesses will benefit from not having to pay high insurance premiums for employees.

The opposition to this issue argues that if we implement a single-payer healthcare system, America could strive more towards the path of socialism (an ideology greatly feared by American conservatives), taxes will rise sky-high, medical services will be rationed, and that healthcare services will be overused. Yet, despite this, I still advocate implementing a universal health care system. Sure, there is some validity in these arguments, yet I cannot fathom how the cons of a single-payer system could ever outweigh the advantages.

More importantly, since we would not be the first country to implement universal healthcare, we could easily study the systems of Australia, Canada, England, Spain, Italy, Finland, Germany, Ireland, Israel, Sweden, Norway, and Portugal, to name a few, and *learn from their mistakes*. Create a better system. Avoid the pitfalls. In this case, being last to the party is to our advantage— opening the way for us to create a far superior system that will serve as the model others would replicate.

To be fair, the United Kingdom, Australia, New Zealand, and Canada do indeed have a few examples of how universal coverage causes countries to ration medical services. According to *Health Care Rationing is Nothing New* by Beatrix Hoffman, these countries use methods such as controlled distribution, price setting, budgeting, and service restrictions to maintain costs. The publicly funded national health care system in the United Kingdom, called the National Health Service

(NHS), sharply restricts access to medical procedures and services such as hip and knee replacements, cataract surgery, and prescription drugs to deal with widespread health issues such as diabetes or arthritis. And overall, average workers in European countries pay much higher taxes than in America. Payroll taxes average 37 percent in Europe, while a common worker in the United States pays around 15 percent according to Paul Roderick Gregory of *Forbes* magazine. But in my opinion, this number is misleading. If one were to combine the percentage of payroll taxes, cost of monthly insurance premiums, and yearly medical costs, the overall percentage of income would more than likely be higher than 37 percent, especially if a person is facing major illness.

As previously mentioned, the United States already has a single-payer health care system in one form. The Department of Veteran's Affairs (VA) provides for eligible military veterans at various medical centers and outpatient clinics, near-comprehensive medical services, and also provides memorial and burial benefits to eligible veterans. According to the U.S. Department of Veterans Affairs, it is the largest integrated health care system, with 1,062 outpatient sites and 172 VA medical centers. According to the United States Census Bureau, there are 18.2 million veterans living in the United States, and more than nine million military veterans are served by the Department of Veterans Affairs.

Although there are exceptions, the Veterans Health Administration is generally a helpful, efficient government institution that—according to CNN'S website as of September 2018—President Donald Trump requested an increase of $12.1 billion over 2018 with an appropriation of $198.6 billion for the department in the 2019 fiscal budget.

My stepfather (whom I refer to as my dad) and two of my grandfathers are all veterans who sing praises about the VA system. This past November, my dad had a blood sugar spike, causing him to pass out while swimming in the ocean. Luckily, my mother was able to pull him to safety, and he was sent to our local hospital instead of the VA hospital several miles away due to its proximity to the beach and the urgency of the situation.

My dad, who served twenty years and earned over twenty medals in the United States Navy, spent a total of *four hours* in the hospital and was sent home the same evening. I was by his side the entire time, and with the exception of a few blood tests and a CAT scan to check for a concussion, he did not receive any treatment for his near drowning. He didn't even occupy a hospital bed overnight, yet our family incurred a bill for $24,000—the equivalent cost of a brand-new car that would provide transportation for ten years, was spent in only four hours.

Within days, bill collectors began calling my dad, mistakenly thinking he was uninsured. Fortunately, my family is in a good economic position and contemplated paying the bill in full to end the harassing calls, but the VA administration quickly picked up the *entire* tab, ending my family's stress immediately. That is when I realized how a single-payer system can be a game changer in the right direction.

After the 2014 political scandal within the Veterans Health Administration, some on the right side of the political spectrum have suggested the VA should compete with private enterprises for veterans' healthcare. They believe that by letting the money follow the veteran, it will create more transparency and more accountability. They believe that by giving vouchers and allowing veterans to decide if they are going to receive care from a private entity or the VA hospital, it would put the power in the hands of the customer. And some would flat out suggest we fully privatize the whole system. Take, for instance, former GOP presidential candidate, Dr. Ben Carson, who now serves as Secretary of Housing and Urban Development. During his 2016 presidential campaign, he supported eradicating all VA medical programs and establishing medical vouchers that any veteran in the country could use to receive private medical services.

There are many flaws with this model, however. The bedrock problem of privatization is that our country would be placing valuable resources into the profit-driven private sector, which would eventually lead to profit-minded competitive advertising that would cause the VA hospital system to die on a vine. It would be like asking people whether they would like a hundred-dollar gift card from Amazon or the post office. In fact, re-directing public resources to the private sector would ensure higher prices, shortcuts in service, and the eradication of profitless treatments.

Also, veterans experience many ailments outside doctors are unfamiliar with, such as burn pit exposure and Post Traumatic Stress Disorder (PTSD). The private sector would be less prepared to help the devastating bodily injuries caused by IED bombs, or to provide the physical and emotional rehabilitation required. Poor veterans with complex needs are expensive patients most for-profit entities would not be happy to serve, no matter how many vouchers might be presented.

Many would agree that veterans do not deserve second-rate health services. They do not deserve homelessness, or the lack of mental health, or the lack of substance abuse treatment. Which is why it is important to note that most of the attacks on the VA during the 2014 scandal may have been fueled by corporate-sponsored affiliates charged with destroying the credibility of a government-run program that provides, for the most part, "excellent care at low cost," as Paul Krugman describes it. This, by some readers, may be highly speculative and reactionary, but as with many other things in our society, financial gain is usually the most logical motive behind any white-collar crime.

The indisputable fact is that the United States of America is the only wealthy, industrialized nation in the world to not ensure free healthcare for all. According to the World Health Organization (WHO) in 2017, the United States spends 18 percent of its Gross Domestic Product (GDP) each year on healthcare, as compared to Turkey, which spends a mere 4.2 percent by providing free healthcare to all of its citizens.

The reason we fear change is that, much like slavery, we have mistakenly built an entire economy dependent on the denial of a human right. If we were to switch overnight to a single-payer system, thousands of people associated with the insurance and pharmaceutical industries will suffer economic loss, and for this reason, we must be careful in the way we implement the new system. But again, like the moral imperative to end slavery, it must be done.

Now, several moderate presidential candidates have suggested we implement both a public and private healthcare option, very similar to what we do with our educational system. This idea sounds wonderful on paper, and it will probably do very well in the polls, but in order for a public healthcare system to work, it must have millions of *healthy* individuals to offset the cost of those who are severely ill. A single-payer healthcare system is the only way our government will have the leverage to keep the costs of prescription drugs, screenings, tests, and treatments very low. And although optional services such as cosmetic surgery will always remain private, the majority of our attention and tax dollars should go to *one* system that we *all* demand must succeed.

Similarly, within the same zip code, both the wealthy and poor share the same publicly funded police department, emergency services, and fire services. No one is advocating we split those services into private and public because the current system works. A public hospital serving all residents will work as well.

Right now, the complexity of a multi-payer basis of our current system is a problem for all Americans. As stated in Bernie Sanders's book *Our Revolution*: "We outspend all other countries on our health, and our medical spending continues to grow faster than the rate of inflation." Furthermore, he found that, "The United States currently spends $3.2 trillion on health care each year—about $10,000 per person."

Ten thousand dollars a person? Where does that money even go?

The United Kingdom—a country with over 67 million people—has implemented in its government a right to healthcare. According to the *U.K. Office for National Statistics*, the United Kingdom spent 9.6 percent of its GDP in 2017 on healthcare, which is nearly half of what America spends. According to the *American Journal of*

Public Health, Canada also spends half as much per capita on providing medical services as the United States.

For years, the WHO ranked French universal healthcare as the best in the world. And despite healthcare costs in France being considered high in European standards, in 2017, it spent 11.3 percent of its GDP on healthcare, or $5,370 per capita. Government-funded agencies cover nearly 80 percent of all health expenditures.

In Switzerland, where healthcare is also universal, there are no free government-provided medical services. Private health insurance is mandatory for all people residing in Switzerland. And despite the fact it spends 12.2 percent of its GDP on healthcare, it's still only the second highest in the world.

Repeatedly, other countries have clearly demonstrated ways to reduce healthcare expenditures, yet politicians often cite the "unimaginable cost" of a single-payer system as being the one barrier to implementation. *Our Revolution* reports that a family of four under Senator Sanders's plan could save over $5,800 just by requiring $466 annually to be paid to a single-payer healthcare plan.

There are other economic benefits to implementing universal healthcare in the United States, yet they are rarely mentioned on the campaign trail.

According to the Institute of Medicine in *Hidden Costs, Value Lost: Uninsurance in America*, our economy loses around $65-$130 billion a year as worker productivity diminishes due to premature deaths and poor health standards among the uninsured. According to a study conducted in March 2012, researchers at the Universities of Pennsylvania and Colorado proposed that insured workers miss an average of 4.7 fewer days than those who are uninsured.

Additionally, establishing a universal right to healthcare would benefit small businesses by significantly reducing employee-related costs. According to "Number of Americans Obtaining Health Insurance through an Employer Declines Steadily Since 2000" by the Robert Wood Johnson Foundation, around 59.5 percent of Americans currently receive medical insurance through their employer. The implementation of a universal right to healthcare in the United States would mean private businesses would no longer be obligated to pay their share for employee healthcare premiums, which the *Business Coalition for Single-Payer Healthcare* claims would reduce employer costs by 10-12 percent overall. Even Vermont Senator Bernie Sanders reported in the previously mentioned book, *Our Revolution*, that the mean yearly costs to the employer for a worker with a family who makes $50,000 annually would decrease from $12,591 to $3,100.

Because of our multi-payer system, the United States is inherently at a competitive disadvantage in the global marketplace. Employers who must share the burden of insurance premiums must charge more for goods sold. It would also encourage and promote entrepreneurship, as many people are hesitant to start their own businesses for dread of losing their health coverage at their existing jobs.

Most importantly, medical bankruptcies would literally disappear if we implemented universal medical coverage.

In February 2019, a CNBC article found that 66.5 percent of all U.S. bankruptcies were tied to medical expenses. The same study found that an estimated 530,000 families turn to bankruptcy each year because of healthcare debt. Millions of people across the country are being harassed by collection agencies about unpaid medical bills, and unlike student loans or credit card debt, the individual did not knowingly sign up for it.

According to a nationwide Bankrate survey, nearly one in three U.S. families decided not to seek medical care for fear of high deductibles and overall costs.

At one time, universal healthcare was a highly popular idea among the American people. In 2018, Reuters conducted a poll that found 70 percent of Americans supported *Medicare for All*. But by the spring of 2020, heavy political advertising convinced the public that it was a deadly move towards socialism, and more moderate presidential candidates were ahead of progressive contenders in the polls.

As a teenager, it is most difficult to watch adults vote against their best interests due to propaganda-like messaging in the mass media. I personally know of a family struggling financially, unable to retire, with a GoFundMe page to raise money for a major health procedure, yet they actively campaign for the one candidate who is dead set against universal healthcare. I have watched people on welfare vote against candidates who advocate raising the minimum wage because of their fear of socialism, and victims of gun violence vote for candidates who are fully backed by the NRA.

This is how bizarre modern elections have become. We have placed identity politics and ideology above direct benefits and common sense.

For example, on March 9, 2020, former Vice President Joe Biden said on MSNBC's *The Last Word with Lawrence O'Donnell* that a single-payer healthcare system would cost 35 trillion dollars a year, and we could never afford that.

Thirty-five trillion dollars a year? That's fourteen trillion dollars more than our annual GDP.

How is it possible that Australia, Canada, England, Spain, Italy, Finland, Germany, Ireland, Israel, Sweden, Norway, and Portugal, can all spend less than 12 percent of their annual GDP on healthcare, yet we will spend 67 percent *more* than our annual GDP?

Why would our universal healthcare cost more than any other country in the world? Aren't we the kings of capitalist innovation? Doesn't that make us the masters of reducing costs and expenses? Apparently, America has done a poor job at teaching math to the average citizen, otherwise everyone would see the fallacy in that reasoning.

In addition, a recent peer-reviewed study by Yale University found that single-payer healthcare would save the United States $450 billion annually, yet on the campaign trail, the cost is always in the "unafford-able" high trillions.

Joe Biden was, however, part of a previous step in the right direction.

―――――

THE PATIENT PROTECTION and Affordable Care Act (PPACA), more commonly known as Obamacare, was a significant attempt toward establishing universal coverage of medical care in the United States.

Although signed by President Barack Obama in 2010, the law's major provisions did not take effect until 2014. According to the Congressional Budget Office, as many as 24 million additional people were covered with insurance through this act, but the mandatory stipulation to obtain health insurance was repealed in 2017 by President Donald Trump.

The reason for this is that insurance premiums for some middle and upper-class families were still outrageously priced, and it was less expensive to pay a one-percent income tax penalty than it was to enroll in the Obamacare sanctioned plan. For example, in 2015, my mother received a quote of $1,666 a month to cover the two of us, coupled with an $8,000 annual deductible, so like millions of other Americans, she decided to pay out of pocket for medical expenses and hope for the best.

Fortunately, today we have a much better and more affordable insurance option called *Tricare* as the result of my stepfather's service in the United States Navy, and our qualification for this military-backed program as his dependents. But had my mother not remarried, we would more than likely be living without health insurance to this day.

Obamacare did, however, slow down the rise of health care costs. According to *The Balance,* in 2004, the price increase of healthcare services was 4 percent. In the year 2016, it was 1.2 percent—a 2.8 percent reduction in price increases. More importantly, the PPACA has prohibited insurance companies from declining coverage for people who have pre-existing conditions. Insurance companies are now unable to drop beneficiaries or increase their premiums if they get sick for whatever reason. Yet this provision is under attack on Capitol Hill nearly every day.

The PPACA also demands that all insurance plans cover essential health benefits, including treatment for addiction, chronic diseases, and mental health issues. This benefits all taxpayers because without these crucial services, many uninsured would end up in the ER, thus charging Medicaid.

In short, Obamacare has done many positive things since its implementation. It has made health insurance more affordable for millions and has given patients a more flexible range of coverage option choices.

But as I write this, the novel Coronavirus, also known as COVID-19, has emerged onto the global scene. In just three months from its discovery, the world has literally closed down. And while other countries are taking action and testing its citizens by the thousands, Congress is at this very moment debating on how we will pay for testing and treatment, because the harsh reality is that 40 percent of all Americans do not even have 400 dollars of emergency funds at their disposal.

Again, our government's duty to protect public health is second only to its duty to provide national security. A global pandemic like COVID-19 is just a dress rehearsal. It's a wake-up call. And if after this crisis, voters fail to recognize the overriding need for *all* people to receive quality healthcare in an effort to keep the entire country healthy, I honestly do not know what it will take.

We took a huge step with the implementation of Obamacare. Now, it is time we make the giant leap toward universal healthcare coverage for all Americans.

CHAPTER 2

Taxation

IN 1909, CONGRESS passed the Sixteenth Amendment to allow the federal government to collect income taxes on both individuals and businesses. With the passage of this Amendment, all companies earning revenue above $5,000 had to pay a one percent uniform tax rate across the country.

Throughout its existence, the corporate tax rate has fluctuated many times. For example, in 1969, it was as high as 52.8 percent. Today, in 2020, the rate is set at 21 percent for all companies. And Americans, throughout corporate tax history, have been divided over whether reducing tax rates for businesses results in the creation of additional jobs, or only increases the profit margins for well-established companies.

The concept of lowering corporate tax rates to create more jobs is more commonly known as "trickle-down economics" or "supply-side economics." It was first popularized by President Ronald Reagan and later promoted by President George Herbert Walker Bush. This concept is still popular today, as President Trump and the Republican-dominated Congress were able to easily pass tax reform legislation with the Tax Cuts and Jobs Act of 2017.

Although I believe the success or failure of trickle-down economics heavily depends on the character and actions of the employers who run the businesses, overall, I believe that there is no proven correlation between job creation and corporate tax rates.

And historically, this has been the case.

According to the Tax Foundation, *Federal Corporate Income Tax Rates, Income Years 1909-2012*, from 1951 to 1969, during the same time period when the corporate income tax rate increased from 42 percent to 50.75 percent, and again to 52.8 percent, the unemployment rate barely increased from 3.3 percent to 3.5 percent. This shows us that when the federal corporate tax rates were at the very highest in this nation's history, our unemployment rate was ironically, also the lowest.

And while acknowledging the fact that recessions and other economic factors also affect unemployment rates, when the top marginal corporate income tax rate was reduced 11 percent, from 46 percent to 35 percent, between the years 1986 and 2011, the unemployment rate increased from 7 percent to 8.9 percent according to the *Bureau of Labor Statistics.*

Therefore, history shows us that cutting taxes for wealthy corporations not only has no impact on job growth, it kills it.

Again, according to the Bureau Labor of Statistics, when the Tax Reform Act of 1986 reduced the top marginal rate from 46 percent to 34 percent, the deficit for the federal government went up from nearly $150 billion to an atrocious $255 billion from the years 1987 to 1993. Recently, with President Trump's Tax Cuts and Jobs Act, the Congressional Budget Office (CBO) approximates the national debt will rise from $16 trillion in the year 2018 to a horrendous $29 trillion in 2028. Additionally, the CBO projects that in 2020, the annual federal deficit will collectively rise above one trillion dollars.

So, how did our 40th president, Ronald Reagan, who served from 1981 to 1989, sell the concept of trickle-down economics to the masses, and become so highly revered by conservatives throughout the country? His image alone embodies the ideological belief that government ought to stay out of personal affairs and keep taxes low for giant corporate executives. "Government is the problem," was his rallying cry to the mega-wealthy. But his brilliance was in convincing the poor, middle class, and upper middle class that by letting corporations keep more of their hard-earned money that they will be more willing to expand and allow average citizens the privilege of working a minimum-wage job.

As a young man who was obviously not around during the eighties, I cannot believe the American public bought this story, particularly since companies are so pressured to show short-term profits on a quarterly basis to their stockholders, and only add jobs and expand to deal with increased product demand, not extra profits lying around in their bank accounts.

Why didn't the average person see this? How could keeping one's employer wealthy be the answer to a worker's personal financial problems?

In addition, President Reagan also passed two major tax reforms that would set the stage for the financial black hole many Americans found themselves sucked into: The Economic Recovery Tax Act of 1981, and the Tax Reform Act of 1986.

According to information released by the Office of Management and Budget (OMB), in 1981, the federal deficit was $79 billion. In 1986, it stood at $221 billion. Furthermore, Reagan's policies ballooned the federal debt from $994 billion in 1981, to $2.9 trillion when his presidency ended in 1989.

And although he lowered the corporate tax rate, he increased taxes for the middle class without them noticing.

According to Paul Krugman in his *New York Times* opinion piece, "The Great Taxer," in 1980, middle-class families with children paid an average of 8.2 percent in income taxes and 9.5 percent in payroll taxes. When 1988 rolled around, their federal income tax reduced to 6.6 percent, but their payroll tax increased to 11.8 percent, which technically accounted for an increase in taxes.

And finally, according to Shelden L. Richman, Reagan pushed through Social Security tax increases of $165 billion over seven years.

What does this all mean?

It means that former Hollywood actor Ronald Reagan used his likable charm to convince the middle class that big government was the enemy, but he did nothing but provide tax cuts to mega-wealthy individuals and giant corporations. He did absolutely nothing to advance the causes of the middle class, except for making capitalism look cool again. Now, I have nothing against President Reagan or his legacy, and I can see why wealthy Republicans and former businessmen like President Trump admire him so much. I just can't see why members of the struggling working class considered him a hero. But to President Reagan's credit, he established the "blue collar billionaire" rulebook that would work again in the 2016 presidential election.

LET'S TAKE A look at the cleanest example of how supply-side economics failed horribly: The Kansas

Experiment. When Republican politician Samuel Dale Brownback was serving as governor of the state of Kansas, he signed Senate Bill HB 2117, one of the biggest income tax cuts in the history of Kansas. Under this ginormous income tax cut for Jayhawkers—which decreased the highest income tax rates by a massive 25 percent and eradicated all income taxes for owners of about 200,000 pass-through businesses in the state—Kansas experienced a 700-million-dollar revenue loss for the entire state according to *The Atlantic*. Brownback believed that economic prosperity for Kansas would come from these massive tax cuts, as more businesses would invest their profits into the economy, and any loss of government tax revenue would solve for itself in the long run. However, the contrary occurred. The viability of the infrastructure and educational system for residents was deeply threatened, and in the year 2017, the Kansas state legislature voted with an overwhelming majority to re-implement the state's tax rates.

Tax cuts failed Kansas. And the economic philosophy that cutting taxes will increase job growth has failed, and is continuing to fail, the entire country as a whole.

And honestly, it is only common sense why reducing corporate income taxes would increase the deficit. A lower tax rate for businesses means less revenue the government would receive, thus diminishing funds for federal programs, investments into the economy, and opportunities that would most certainly spur job creation.

Earlier this year, before the COVID-19 pandemic tanked our productivity, American corporations were sitting on record-breaking amounts of money. For example, Apple corporation was the first company to reach a trillion-dollar market capitalization. According to its first-quarter 2019 earnings report, it had over $245 billion sitting in cash. That's right—245 billion dollars sitting in bank accounts as emergency reserves, not being used to add jobs, or open new stores, or hand out rebates to its customers. Although some major companies like Amazon have used their near zero corporate tax rate to increase minimum wage for its workers, in general, the concept of low corporate tax rates directly resulting in bigger paychecks for lower-income workers is flawed.

In addition, Moody's Investor Service conducted a report and found that non-financial companies based in the United Sates held onto a staggering $1.77 trillion in profits during the year 2016—an increase of the previous years' historically high $1.68 trillion. Corporations could have invested into the U.S. economy to produce more jobs, but they know that unsubstantiated expansion without the demand for products or services is business suicide.

President Barack Obama summed up many people's frustration when he stated in a July 22, 2009 press conference that, "At a time when everybody's getting hammered, they're making record profits."

More importantly, hysteria about raising the federal corporate income tax rate is also unfounded because perfectly legal loopholes, huge deductions, and the ability to spread out massive financial losses taken early in a company's growth over a number of years, allows many corporations to contribute less than what is required by statutory law.

According to Patricia Cohen's *New York Times* article, "Profitable Companies, No Taxes: Here's How They Did It," between the years of 2008-2015, nearly 40 percent of the 258 profitable companies within the Fortune 500 paid zero taxes for a minimum of one year over that time span. In addition, Fareed Zakaria, author of *Complexity Equals Corruption*, found that out of the 500 largest cap companies—corporations with a market capitalization value of greater than $10 billion in the Standard & Poor (S&P) stock index—39 companies paid less than 10 percent in taxes.

It's pure and simple: trickle-down economic policies are detrimental to the middle class. Ironically, the poorest counties and states receiving the most government assistance in America are also the most conservative. Another example of how people vote against their best interest. And according to the *New York Times* article, "Where Government is a Dirty Word, but its Checks Pay the Bills," by Eduardo Porter, GOP presidential nominee Donald Trump won seven out of the ten states in which government transfers account for the largest share of income.

NOW, LET'S TAKE the example of the people of Harlan County, Kentucky, as a conservative county that typically votes against their best interest.

According to the Bureau of Economic Analysis, Harlan County is the fifth most dependent place in the country in terms of receiving federal financial assistance. In the year 2016, Medicaid, Social Security, welfare, and earned-income tax credits comprised 54 percent of the income of Harlan County's 26,000 residents. That is a 26 percentage-point increase from 1990.

According to the same *New York Times* article, more than 10,000 people in Harlan receive food stamps. And about 13 percent of Harlan's residents also receive Social Security disability benefits. Yet despite this, nearly 90 percent of residents in Harlan voted for President Trump in 2016, who stands clearly against socialism, welfare, and high corporate taxes to benefit the poor.

Now, my biggest questions for the roughly 23,400 residents of Harlan County, Kentucky, who supported President Trump in the 2016 election are these: What was the defining issue that led you to vote Republican? Did you take into consideration the performance of tax cuts over the years, and how it directly or indirectly affected you? Do you realize that being dependent on the government to assist your basic needs is the basic principle behind socialism, a concept vehemently opposed by the Republican party? Finally, and most importantly, do you consider the government to be your greatest enemy or your biggest ally?

By no means do I wish to sound disrespectful to the residents of Harlan County. I have never stepped foot in the great state of Kentucky, but I hope to visit it one day on the campaign trail. I just sincerely want to know how a party who openly prioritizes the preservation of wealth among the fortunate could look so attractive to those so far from it.

Just how did the Republican party do it? What did they say? What was the magic word?

Or should I ask, what was the magic *social issue* adopted by the Republican party that blinded you to the economic programs designed to keep you in the bottom ninety-nine percent?

The institution of government is one of the greatest cornerstones of society. It exists to serve the people within its jurisdiction. It is the safeguard of all Americans and their health, wealth, and well-being. In some cases, and when the market fails you, government is also the hand that feeds you.

If the residents of Harlan County answered my questions honestly, they may come to the realization that trickle-down economics never benefited anyone but the top ten to twenty percent. They may realize their voting strategy based purely on social issues cut off the lifeline to their local economy. They may realize they failed to recognize a candidate who could have delivered them from generational poverty, all because of fear that his or her ideas were "Un-American."

I pray the residents of Harlan County take a good, hard look at what their community truly needs this next election cycle, and elect the best candidates who will help their economy *first*.

ANOTHER ISSUE THAT should be addressed in this chapter is the growth of the modern tax code. In short, the amount of regulations regarding taxation in this country is ridiculous, and we need to simplify it.

In March 2017, Republican members of the House Ways and Means Committee found the tax code nearly tripled in length over the previous three decades. In 2015, the Tax Foundation found that the total length of the tax code now consists of more than 10 million words versus 1955, when that number was just 1.4 million words. The best part is that a group of bureaucrats are profiting from this monstrosity, but more on that issue later.

Some have proposed that a valid solution to our taxation issue here in America is to replace the federal income tax program with a national sales tax program. Under this system, we would simplify the tax code by slashing thousands of complicated, unnecessary regulations imposed onto the American public. This program would furthermore force all members of society—whether on the top or bottom of socioeconomic standing—to contribute to public financing. Various sources suggest that unlike the current tax structure in America, the implementation of this new system would allow all citizens to control how much they pay in taxes. Everything in this new structure would be controlled at the point of sale, which would not only eliminate bureaucracy, but also increase the productivity of businesses and workers that would overall raise revenue for the American government.

Since a lot more people would be impacted by the transformation into this new system, additional money would be raised to satisfy the needs of various Americans. People would not "feel" the tax increase when paid only a few dollars at a time. With this money, we would be able to invest more into domestic programs—to truly invest in America. And with a national sales tax structure, everyone would benefit as a whole, and we can finally be equal in how we distribute taxation.

However, there are many downsides to implementing a national sales tax program. In order to achieve what the program is trying to accomplish, the plan advocates to defund and dismantle the IRS, and repeal the Sixteenth Amendment to the Federal Constitution. These procedures are, frankly, politically impractical and time-consuming. Administering the collection of taxes when consumers buy products would also require the establishment of a new agency, thus imposing more governmental bureaucracy to oversee the American public.

More importantly, a sales tax would be regressive instead of progressive, disproportionally affecting lower-income families. Proponents of a retail sales tax program have in the past proposed instating an income rebate that might make up for the financial losses inflicted upon poor and middle-class people. Again, while worth considering, this idea is impractical and a bit complicated. Imagine what would happen if another viral pandemic hit our country, forcing all businesses, restaurants, and bars to close down for months again. Or if a foreign adversary took down our electricity grid for 90 days. How would we generate revenue for our government if no sales transactions were taking place?

I think a national sales tax program is actually a wonderful idea to raise *additional* revenue should our country need to pay for programs like free college, or free daycare, but it should not replace our existing federal income tax system. Perhaps if we implemented a simple, flat-rate income tax based on income level, in addition to a national sales tax of three to five percent, we would be able to eliminate the confusing tax code and raise even more money than before.

So why does Congress fight to keep such a complicated tax system?

Over many years, Congress has altered the tax code to include several loopholes and roundabout laws that essentially allow giant corporations and wealthy individuals to avert paying taxes that would benefit society as a whole. According to a *Fortune* magazine website article, an Institute on Taxation and Economic Policy (ITEP) analysis found that of the Fortune 500 companies that filed their taxes in 2018, 60 paid no federal income tax. Yet, all of them were profitable in that year. According to my source, "The total U.S. income of the top 60 companies including Amazon, Chevron, General Motors, Delta, Halliburton, and IBM was more than 79 billion dollars and the effective tax rate was -5 percent. On the average, they got tax refunds." The ITEP also found that these companies should have paid a collective $16.4 billion in federal income taxes based on the new Tax Cuts and Jobs Act of 2017 rate of 21 percent. But not surprisingly, they, in reality, received a tax rebate of $4.3 billion.

Now, to be clear, I sincerely admire self-made millionaires and billionaires. I obviously strive to become one in adulthood by working hard and investing my earnings wisely. The ability to achieve financial success is one of the greatest things about our country. In fact, my mother has often said that instead of trying to change the rules of the game, it is much easier to go out there, find the opportunities, drive oneself, and "just *be* the one percent."

While I most certainly believe millionaires and billionaires should not be punished for their wealth, or be forced to pay enormous taxes upon previously taxed money (such as 80 percent capital gains taxes or ridiculous inheritance taxes), I do feel corporations should be limited in the number of years they can spread their losses and collect tax incentives.

The beauty of our free-enterprise system is that *anyone* in America, with the proper amount of determination, smarts, and resiliency, can achieve big things. I most wholeheartedly believe entrepreneurs are essential to the American economy, and we should encourage investment in the financial sector. I admire people like Steve Jobs, Elon Musk, and Jeff Bezos for positively changing the global zeitgeist in many ways. Yet, the taxation system we currently have in place is grossly unsustainable. More importantly, we have placed invisible barriers of educational disparity and information hoarding from the lower socioeconomic classes in an effort of keeping the status quo in place.

Tell me, why don't we teach *all* third-graders the power of compounding interest? And that if a Starbucks employee saved a solid ten percent of his or her modest income every year from the age of 16, that they would be practically guaranteed to be a millionaire by retirement age? Or that the most reliable maker of wealth for the common man is through long-term investing in the U.S. stock market? Why haven't inner city mothers demanded these "wealth concepts" be taught to their children? It's because they don't know wealth creation is a skill that can be *learned*.

There is a science to getting rich, and there is a formula for staying wealthy. UPS worker Theodore Johnson never made more than $14,000 a year and died worth $70 million. Boxer Mike Tyson earned $400 million dollars before the age of 40 and went broke in 2007. Can you guess which person bought his wife a two-million-dollar gold bathtub? I bet you can. Truth is, there are *teachable* financial principles in place that explain how this happens, and the working class is being left in the dark on purpose, forced to deal with survival issues instead.

So, is it radical to propose that a man who earns nearly $2,500 a second should be obligated by society to pay his fair share of taxes so that we may distribute enough resources to help everyone in America climb the socioeconomic ladder? Perhaps our paralyzing fear of terms like "redistribution of wealth" scare us from implementing minor stopgaps in our beloved capitalist economy that would ensure capitalism would thrive for generations to come.

I mean, as long as everyone has sufficient food, shelter, lottery tickets, alcohol, drugs, and fulfilling entertainment, no one will feel the need to come together and form a revolution. Even history taught us that it took a great food shortage before the French realized things needed to change, so as long as the struggling working class gets their tasty, fast-food dollar meal options, capitalism will survive. And that helps me sleep at night, but we need not wait for a call for revolution to make our existing capitalist system even better.

———————

THE U.S. GOVERNMENT, from The Great Depression to the 1970s, aggressively pushed for more regulation of corporate activity and rightfully imposed high tax rates for the well-to-do. Then, in the 1980s, Ronald Reagan led the American public into believing that "government is not the solution to the problem; government *is* the problem," as I have previously mentioned.

So, what were the effects of government flexing some muscle in monitoring Wall Street? According to Senator Elizabeth Warren's book *This Fight Is Our Fight*, the bottom 90 percent of America earned 70 percent of all income growth, while the top 10 percent received 30 percent. America during this time period invested in opportunity for all citizens, which included safeguarding seniors and vulnerable Americans from financial misery, allocating money on several infrastructure projects which produced quality jobs, and helping to preserve the hopes and dreams of millions of Americans nationwide. The United States was a nation where more for me did not mean less for you.

From 1980 to 2020, the top ten percent of America received nearly one hundred percent of income growth, leaving essentially nothing for the rest of the citizenry.

Just let that sink in for a moment. Ninety percent of the people had zero income growth for the past 40 years. Shouldn't this be our "let them eat cake" moment?

But instead, big corporations have found a way to convince the American people that cake was the enemy, not a corporate-backed political system.

Taxation is directly linked to wealth distribution and income inequality. While the rate of inflation is skyrocketing, the wealthy are simply not investing in their enterprises the way Republicans would like us to think. Thus, wages are stagnant, though the price of essential goods are rising. I will further elaborate on this point in an upcoming chapter.

The simple fact of the matter is that our tax system must be based on a progressive model; the amount of taxes you pay should be based upon how much you earn or how much you own. In layman's terms, we must raise the corporate and personal income tax rate for *all* Americans to help finance essential government services that benefit the whole country.

I believe the most appropriate path forward is one that aligns more toward what former New York City Mayor Michael Bloomberg recently proposed. While I do think that the Trump Tax Cuts have proven ineffective in spurring sustainable economic growth, I also do not believe that Senator Bernie Sanders's or Senator Elizabeth Warren's wealth tax proposals are what America needs at this moment. It is crucial that we return to implementing a progressive tax code system that forces all Americans to pay their fair share while also allowing economic innovation to prosper within the nation.

The first step we need to take in actually reforming the tax code is to completely eliminate several loopholes that allow the wealthy to avoid paying their appropriated amount of taxes at the expense of the working middle class. We also need to end the absurd complexity of the tax code that fosters government corruption and incompetence. We need a tax system that requires all members to contribute financially for the well-being of all of society, and—at the same time—is easy, fair, and simple.

Thus, we need to raise the corporate tax rate from its current level of 21 percent back to a clean 30 percent. In 2017, just before the implementation of the Tax Cuts and Jobs Act took place, the United States had the fourth highest corporate income tax rate in the world, at 35 percent. So, a five-percent drop would still be attractive. We must also stop the practice of allowing companies to spread their initial investment losses over many years. As soon as a company turns a profit, it should be paying taxes. It's as simple as that.

It is also pivotal that we change the top-tier income rate from 37 percent to 40 percent, for individual tax-payers making more than $518,400 per year. This three-percent increase would equate to roughly $18,000 for an individual making $600,000 a year, which is significantly less than the ten-percent or $60,000 tithe a church may expect to receive to help the community. And if we remove the high cost of monthly health insurance premiums, it will actually be less overall spending for the top five percent of income earners.

Now, in order to make sure individuals abide by the law, I think it is pivotal we increase funding for the IRS to help combat tax evasion and the transferring of company funds to foreign tax havens, which foster a large number of white-collar crimes. Additionally, we should impose a one-time tax penalty on people who defect their citizenship in order to avoid U.S. taxes, as Massachusetts Senator Elizabeth Warren proposed during her bid for the 2020 Democratic Nomination.

IN CONCLUSION, IT is the universal obligation of all Americans to contribute their fair share of taxes to help pay for the most fundamental public services. It is absolutely imperative—in order for us to grow as a nation—that the very wealthiest members of our society pay taxes in order to help fund essential government services such as education, infrastructure, and affordable housing. This is not an obligation; it is a *privilege* to pay taxes. Because if you are lucky enough to have to write a check on April 15th instead of receiving one, you are doing rather well in our survival-of-the-fittest economy.

Most importantly, I believe we need to reverse the Tax Cuts and Jobs Act of 2017 that is delving us deeper into financial insolvency. The nonpartisan Tax Policy Center found that more than 60 percent of the tax savings went to people in the top 20 percent of the income ladder. Secretary of the Treasury Department Steven Mnuchin, mislead the American people when he declared that "the tax plan will pay for itself with economic growth." The stock market did indeed reach all-time highs under President Trump's administration. But for the 149 million Americans who do *not* invest in the stock market, this meant diddly squat.

However, there is simply no way trickle-down economics can stimulate the economy when, according to the National Public Radio (NPR), corporate tax revenues fell 31 percent in the first year after the tax reform bill was passed.

And now, with our economy flirting with a depression, our plan for recovery will need aggressive measures to invest in future generations and spark real economic growth, starting with the need to implement FDR-like federal programs (like the Green New Deal), that can only be funded by a reversal of Trump-implemented tax laws.

CHAPTER 3

Social Security

SOCIAL SECURITY, MORE formally known as Old-Age, Survivors, and Disability Insurance (OASDI), accounted for $945 billion or 24 percent of total U.S spending in 2017 and has become the largest single government-provided program around the globe, with an annual budget of over a trillion dollars according to *A Summary of the 2017 Annual Reports* by the Social Security and Medicare Boards of Trustees.

Social Security is a social insurance program that covers retirement, survivors', and disability benefits. For retirement services, it provides a basic, universal monthly income for people starting around the ages of 62 to 67, depending on the level of benefits selected and birth year.

President Franklin Delano Roosevelt (FDR) signed the Social Security act in the year 1935, and it has been amended throughout the years to engulf many social insurance and welfare programs. The program is funded mostly through payroll taxes, which are taxes levied on both employees and employers, calculated as a percentage of salary.

There are many different types of payroll taxes. The two payroll taxes associated with Social Security are FICA, the Federal Insurance Contributions Act tax, and SECA, the Self-Employed Contributions Act tax. The ones collected by the Internal Revenue Service (IRS) and the two Social Security Trust Funds, are the Survivors Insurance Trust Fund and the Federal Disability Insurance Fund, and the Old-Age and Survivors Insurance Trust Fund.

For the most part, all legal residents working in America must have an individual Social Security number. This has been the case since the implementation of Social Security, since it is requested by a large number of corporations and businesses, and many people who do not work also receive benefits and have a card number.

In short, Social Security is a safety net—an idea that if everyone pooled a fraction of their income, our country would be able to protect the elderly and save them from poverty. It is a core fundamental program that, according to the Center on Budget and Policy Priorities, is estimated to have reduced the poverty rate from nearly

40 percent to under 10 percent for Americans aged 65 years and older. It is the last financial line of defense for the old and retired. And to promote the idea that we should privatize this uniquely American program is to promote the demise of it.

So, why is a fourteen-year-old concerned with the fate of social security?

Because in 2018, the trustees of the Social Security Trust Fund projected the federally administered program will become fiscally insolvent by the year 2034, when I will only be 29 years old.

Many on the right side of the political spectrum propose replacing the government- administered system with a partial privatization, which would allow workers to handle their personal retirement funds through private investment accounts. They believe these personal financial accounts would give retired workers greater returns on investments than what the current Social Security system could provide, and that overall, privatization would help restore the program's fiscal solvency.

Due to a lower birthrate and an aging United States population, the ratio between retirees and workers is diminishing, thus the funds for retirees in the future is shrinking. For instance, in the year 2013, the estimated ratio between young workers and elderly recipients was 2.8 to 1 according to the Social Security Administration. In 1940, that ratio was 159 to 1!

Social Security is quickly becoming a fiscal nightmare, and privatization is becoming more appealing every day. However, there are four main reasons why privatization of Social Security would be an awful idea.

The first, and perhaps the most important reason, is that putting Social Security into private hands will undermine the entire purpose of the program: a safety net designed to guarantee retirement income for every American. The reasoning behind this claim is that the U.S. stock market—which can be very volatile—will have peoples' retirement funds placed within its whims.

In 2008, during the financial crisis that struck America, the Dow Jones Industrial Average fell 33.8 percent, the S&P 500 fell 38.5 percent, and the NASDAQ index sank a staggering 40.5 percent. Yesterday, the DOW fell nearly 3,000 points—the worst day since 1987—causing the Fed to slash interest rates to zero due to the Coronavirus pandemic.

Now imagine if your *sole* retirement fund was subject to this level of short-term turmoil. How secure would you feel about your future? All retired Americans deserve a basic, guaranteed income they will not have to fear losing or diminishing.

Second reason: bureaucracy in the government would increase, not decrease, if we privatize Social Security. Proponents of privatizing Social Security like to talk about how placing the management of retirement funds into the hands of private companies would heavily reduce needless spending, red tape, and bureaucracy in our government. That's just ridiculous.

First of all, the government would need to fill a multi-trillion-dollar hole left by transitioning from public to private accounts, and yet still provide benefits to current recipients under the program. This hole would significantly increase the national debt of the United States.

For example, President George Walker Bush's plan to partially privatize Social Security would have, according to Bloomberg Business, made "Washington borrow at least $160 billion a year in early years," forcing the national debt to rise nearly 40 percent. Furthermore, government bureaucracy would grow significantly if we privatized Social Security. Logically, more government bureaucracy would expand as tens of thousands of people would need to be educated, hired, and sufficiently trained to manage the financial accounts of millions of Americans. They would also need to explain to millions of people the way financial systems work. And according to various sources, in the year 2014, the costs of administrating the current Social Security system were less than one percent of all revenues.

According to *The Balance*, placing any portion of the Social Security trust into the private world, would doom the system, as Social Security has liabilities that must be paid, and the earnings of people who pay into Social Security help cover these liabilities.

Third reason: many Americans are not educated in the financial field.

In 2015, *USA Today* conducted a survey and found that less than 40 percent of Americans know the annual percentage rate (APR) on their primary credit card. The same survey found that only 45 percent are even informed on what a credit card evaluates. According to a 2009 study conducted by researchers Olivia S. Mitchell and Annamaria Lusdardi of Dartmouth College, only 50 percent of people over the age of 50 could answer simple economic questions on issues such as inflation and compound interest.

Now, how can we trust all Americans to make wise financial decisions for themselves? We can't. At least not until we start teaching wealth management every year, staring in the third grade. Until then, there needs to be a financial safety net to provide for all Americans, no matter what their knowledge is concerning economics and monetary matters.

Century Foundation conducted an analysis in the year 2005 and found that under President George Walker Bush's proposal to overturn Social Security to free enterprise, if payroll taxes were diverted to personal accounts, it would have caused benefits to be slashed by nearly 44 percent by 2052. This was the number before the 2008 financial crisis, and at the time of this writing, no one knows how deep the 2020 financial turmoil will impact this projection as well.

In sum, the essential bedrock of Social Security would be eroded significantly for Americans who do not have the knowledge or resources necessary to retire themselves with no other government assistance. The last line of financial defense would be dissolved.

Finally, the fourth reason: we already have a privatized retirement structure in the United States. We have tax-advantaged accounts, 401(k) accounts, IRA accounts, and many other privatized retirement vehicles that citizens have primary control over. In addition, nearly everyone has the ability to open up a trading account online (once minimum investment requirements are met), arrange for automatic deductions to be taken from their paychecks, and have total control over their investment decisions to create a private retirement account. This is a perfect complement to Social Security but by no means replaces it.

As previously stated, while privatization of Social Security sounds like an appealing idea, it could force retired workers to fall deep within a financial hole. According to *The Balance*, while the investment value of 401(k)s are rising, accounts owned by people aged 65 or older have a median value of about $60,000. If a person lives to age 85, that means they can only draw approximately $3,000 a year. The average Social Security benefit is $1,360 per person, so when you do the math, that equates to $20,000 in yearly income. That is not a suitable income for an average American. And logically, why would we privatize a government program that guarantees a basic pension while workers already have control over their private retirement funds?

That's right. Americans already have a choice.

Therefore, the argument that privatizing Social Security would give retired workers more financial freedom is invalid, as there is no justifiable reason to privatize Social Security. Americans must have a fundamental safety net to provide essential financial protection. And while I acknowledge the fact that Social Security is becoming fiscally insolvent, privatization is not the answer. Therefore, we must cut wasteful government spending, reverse Trump's corporate tax rate cut, and progressively raise the upper brackets of personal income taxes each year as needed to make up the difference.

Our last line of financial defense must stand tall.

CHAPTER 4

Tariffs, Trade, and Automation

OUR ACTIONS WITHIN the realm of foreign trade have a greater impact on our national economy than most Americans think. In 2019, the U.S. Chamber of Commerce reported that international trade supports as many as 39 million American jobs—a number that has doubled from 1992 to 2017. So, when President Trump made it a priority during his first term to review and revise nearly all of our existing foreign trade deals, economists around the country braced themselves and prepared for a drastic change in the way we do business around the world.

The Peterson Institute for International Economics (PIIE) estimates that a 131-billion-dollar annual increase in incomes were lost due to Trump's withdrawal from the Trans-Pacific-Partnership (TPP) trade pact in 2017. And although he has signed a "Phase 1 China Trade Deal" in 2020 designed to reduce his previously higher tariff rates from 15 percent to 7.5 percent on 112 billion dollars' worth of goods to stop the trade war he initiated, the spirit behind his trade policies may have implications that last for generations.

The North American Free Trade Agreement (NAFTA), was a trade agreement between the three nations of North America—the United States, Canada, and Mexico—from the years 1994-2020. This trade deal impacted nearly half a billion people during this time.

According to *The Balance*, trade among the nations of North America increased four-fold over this time period as it primarily repealed tariffs and created nearly five million jobs in the United States.

Overall, during the NAFTA years, wages have risen, the costs of automotive products have gone down, government contracts have been more competitive in their bidding, and services—such as U.S. healthcare and finance exports—have increased. Foreign direct investment (FDI) has increased as businesses contributed nearly $452 billion in Canada and Mexico as well.

According to the U.S. Bureau of Labor Statistics, under the NAFTA Agreement, the average price of new cars has risen only about 7 percent, in comparison to the average cost increase of 86 percent for all other items, including energy and food, since the 1990s.

For instance, if one compares a 2018 Chevy Suburban, which has new technological features such as a backup camera or remote engine start, to a 1993 Chevy Suburban, we can see that the 2018 version of the car only costs $4,844 more when the price is adjusted for inflation. In 25 years, the prices for these cars has stayed fairly consistent, which is an extraordinary accomplishment made possible primarily through free trade.

Now, under the previous guidelines of NAFTA, the components of a car needed to be at least 62.5 percent sourced from the North American continent to be tariff-free (tariffs are taxes imposed on imported goods from other countries). Cars manufactured with less than 62.5 percent of parts sourced from North America must endure a 2.5 percent tariff.

So, if NAFTA worked so well, why did we replace it?

The reason why politicians and many Americans vehemently opposed NAFTA was due to perception. According to the Congressional Research Office, under former NAFTA guidelines, a typical car made in the United States cost nearly $1,200 more than a car made in the country of Mexico. Therefore, companies were moving their manufacturing plants to Mexico due to labor and production costs being cheaper, which is why people felt NAFTA directly affected jobs here in the United States.

The PIIE found that nearly one-third of all manufacturing jobs disappeared in the United States from the years 1994-2013, a nineteen-year span since the establishment of NAFTA. This has been the opposite for Mexico, as the same source found that the number of manufacturing jobs there have grown by roughly the same amount.

While I think the newly passed United States-Mexico-Canada Agreement (USMCA) has some major positive provisions, I quite frankly hold the view that NAFTA was a fair-trade deal that served as a scapegoat for a much bigger economic crisis. I will further elaborate on this point later.

In the meantime, we need to advocate for higher environmental, labor, and safety standards when negotiating international trade deals. U.S. workers must receive government assistance to adjust to job displacement caused by trade wars and bad deals. Former Colorado Governor John Hickenlooper has proposed creating a system of Individual Security Accounts (ISAs), which will be mobile accounts tied to particular individuals, funded pre-tax with a combination of government, worker, and employer contributions, with continuing employer and employee contributions similar to current IRAs. He proposed the Secretary of Labor would designate certain geographic areas that were negatively impacted by trade deals and devote more pre-tax funds to the ISAs of workers who reside in these places in order to help fund their training, relocation, and other steps to adjustment.

According to Ward Automotive Center for Automotive Research, car production increased in the United States, Mexico, and Canada since the implementation of NAFTA. And the manufacturing job losses experienced by many Americans should not be blamed on NAFTA, but rather the advancement of automation.

The PIIE stated that only 5 percent of sizable layoffs can be blamed for the United States freely trading with Mexico. And this new deal presented to all three of North America's countries, the USMCA might even jeopardize more American jobs in the future.

For instance, one thing that is different about NAFTA and the USMCA is that under USMCA guidelines, 75 percent—instead of 62.5 percent—of a car's parts must be sourced from the North American continent to avoid a 2.5 percent tariff being imposed.

According to the Center for Automotive Research, 46 to 125 American car models that met NAFTA's 62.5 percent North American parts requirement would fail to qualify under the new USMCA regulations. In light of these new regulations, automakers would need to either pay the 2.5 percent tariff set by the USMCA, or increase production costs in switching their vendor sources for auto-making materials. Either way, the consumer is affected, as the prices of American-made cars could increase up to $2,200 per vehicle according to various sources, causing the relocation of car manufacturing companies to other countries.

The three North American countries have already signed the agreement, and at the time of this writing, it is expected to go into effect as of July 1, 2020 (unless postponed by the Coronavirus pandemic currently unfolding). The agreement does, indeed, have widespread bipartisan support, and Democrats were victorious in revising certain sections in the deal that advance progressive causes. Although I generally saw nothing wrong with the previous NAFTA agreement, there are some provisions in USMCA that are beneficial.

For instance, according to my sources, the USMCA stipulates that 40 to 45 percent of automobile parts must be made by workers who are paid a minimum $16.00 per hour by 2023. Mexico has also agreed to grant stronger protections for its workers, including making it easier for them to unionize as laborers.

The Office of the United States Trade Representative has also touted the agreement as expanding market access for American food and agricultural products, which directly benefits farmers. The agreement also implements new guidelines for intellectual property violations. And while some conservation groups have lamented the agreement doesn't go far enough in environmental regulations, the deal does provide several protections for marine species, stipulations to improve air quality, and supports measures to establish sustainable forest management, as well as other things.

Overall, I think the USMCA is a good deal. However, I am still disappointed with the new tariff law that will negatively impact American consumers. But at least this agreement takes our country farther away from the political concept of *protectionism*—an economic philosophy that advocates for the shielding of a country's domestic industries from foreign competition by taxing imports or implementing other isolationist measures to protect them.

Protectionism does nothing but increase economic hostilities between countries, and history has proven many times that it does not result in economic growth for any country that embraces it. Take, for instance, the political mishaps of President Benjamin Harrison.

———

BENJAMIN HARRISON, WHO served as the 23rd President of the United States from 1889-1893, was elected in 1888 as a pro-tariff Republican. Under his administration, the McKinley Tariff Act was passed by Congress and signed into law. This legislation "led to the highest tariffs in American history up to that time," as reported in 1988 by the *Chicago Tribune*.

Consumer prices began to immediately rise after the implementation of President Harrison's law, and cheaper foreign products were nearly inaccessible. The American public was not happy with this drastic change in the cost of living. As a result, the GOP lost the House Majority in 1890 and the presidency in 1892.

More recently, the idea of protectionism creating more problems than it solves is best exemplified under President Trump's recent tariff increase on steel and aluminum. As of 2019, steel and aluminum originating from other countries are now subject to 25 percent and 10 percent tariffs respectively, and in turn, other countries raised *their* tariffs on items imported from the United States.

This, ladies and gentlemen, is how you start a trade war.

According to *The Age*, China has implemented tariffs equal to the 34 billion dollars in tariffs the United States imposed on it. Countries, such as Canada, have also reacted negatively to the Trump tariffs in the past. And there is a general consensus among economists that these protectionist tariffs do not help the welfare of Americans, and whatever benefit shared between a few home-based aluminum and steel producers, quickly disappeared.

Any gain from a tariff increase is suppressed when the price of steel increases and producers who are heavily dependent on the output of foreign trade partners must pay more and extract more resources to produce their product. For example, the U.S. beer industry was greatly affected by this recent trade war. According to *The Hill*, Jim McGreevey, president of a national trade association representing the interests of companies that produce and import beer within the United States called The Beer Institute, estimates that Trump's economic policies have put at least 20,000 industry-dependent jobs in jeopardy.

In 2017, The Beer Institute found that brewers spent nearly 5 billion dollars on beer cans alone, half of which was used to purchase aluminum. That means a ten percent tariff on this vital material increased costs by $250 million in 2019 alone!

Another example is the Alcoa Corporation. *Bloomberg* reported that the aluminum-product producer slashed its profit forecast by nearly $500 million due to the aluminum trade war with China.

In addition, The Cato Institute listed on its website over 200 cases of companies and private enterprises suffocating due to the protectionist policies of the Trump administration.

Furthermore, the Trump tariffs have also economically impacted the auto industry that he promised would be strengthened under his presidency. In 2018, General Motors announced it would shut down plants and cut more than 14,000 jobs, citing the increase in steel tariffs as the main factor for this decision.

In fact, recent reports found that Trump's tariffs are only raising the trade deficit. A *Washington Post* article cited the increased deficit of $621 billion is nearly 25 percent larger than the trade deficit recorded in 2016 under President Obama, which was $502 billion.

American protectionist policies cause foreign nations to raise tariffs in response, which is harmful economically to all countries in terms of jobs. Yet despite this, the Global Trade Alert has found that since the financial crisis of 2007-2008, the United States of America has enacted over 1,000 protectionist measures—the most in the world since then.

Somehow, we must balance the penalties of protectionism while, at the same time, guarding our country from the pitfalls of free and open trade. The government must obtain the necessary resources from the private sector to retrain and financially salvage American victims of job attrition. We must kill monopolies that negatively affect the integrity of the common worker or small business. We must invest in essential societal institutions such as education and healthcare to advance the disadvantaged. These are the proper measures to ensure every American benefits from the positive aspects of free trade.

With that said, an even bigger problem than foreign trade wars is the advancement of automation and the scars left on the American worker. To put it bluntly, we must enact measures now to ensure human jobs stay viable, or my generation will be facing unprecedented issues of unemployment never before seen in human history.

Our greatest achievement as humans will turn out to be our biggest downfall: the invention of Artificial Intelligence.

In 2017, *Ball State* reports that only 13 percent of jobs were lost in manufacturing that year due to free trade, while the rest were eradicated from advancements in technology. This is a scary statistic, as I found numerous other sources that claim automation—not free or protectionist trade—is the number one job killer coming down the pipeline.

We already see it everywhere in America. From Walmart to McDonalds, automated warehouses, self-serving kiosks, and self-checkout machines are replacing tasks that people need to fulfill in order to justify their positions. Automation is also the reason why 2020 Presidential Candidate, Andrew Yang, proposed his "Freedom Dividend," which is essentially a universal basic income of $1,000 a month to every U.S. citizen over the age of 18. I will further elaborate my thinking on this in a later chapter, but clearly, the government's need to do something to combat automation is quickly becoming an issue.

Unfortunately, we may even need to financially penalize any corporation who decides to use automated labor over human flesh. We need to actively de-incentivize corporations from trying to eliminate expenses by completely changing the dynamics of their workforce. And although this may be the most anti-capitalist move our country has ever made, I sadly think it will be necessary for our overall survival.

Remember my earlier reference to the French Revolution? How it took a severe food shortage before peasants formed together to storm the Bastille? Well, for us, it may be lack of employment. Not general unemployment, or even high unemployment during times of crisis, but a systemic lack of jobs in disproportion to the population, will undoubtedly cause a revolution no world leader will ever want to face.

Automation could lead to the death of capitalism.

Let's not wait twenty years for this to become a major problem. Our government must implement strategies now to discourage the use of technologies that increase short-term profits while slowly eroding the need for human laborers.

CHAPTER 5

Climate Change

HANDS DOWN, CLIMATE change—or climate *crisis* as Greta Thunberg prefers to call it—is the single most important issue facing my generation, yet according to my personal observations, it received less than 30 minutes of discussion in the 30.5 televised hours of the 2020 National Democratic Debates. Even the lack of traction of the fourth-largest political party in our country, The Green Party, is a shocking example of how few Americans know exactly what the scientific community is saying.

Young people—both conservative and liberal alike— are flabbergasted by the fact that the mere *existence* of a climate change crisis is even a debatable issue among older generations who will most certainly not be around to feel the effects of it. This is incredibly alarming, particularly since the rest of the world agrees with the hard data released by the Intergovernmental Panel on Climate Change (IPCC) that states we have roughly eight to ten years left to clean up our act or we will suffer the end of humanity.

That's a catchy statement, indeed.

And with President Trump's recent withdrawal from the 195-nation climate deal made in 2015, commonly known as The Paris Agreement, this issue clearly needs to move center stage and be attacked with the sort of intensity, rigor, and discipline that puts our long-term survival ahead of short-term economics—essentially mirroring our country's response to the Coronavirus outbreak of 2020.

So, what are we doing in the area of climate change?

The Green New Deal is more than a Democratic-backed economic package, it is a movement spawned by a congressional resolution that spells out a comprehensive plan for tackling climate change. As the National Wildlife Federation reported, sea levels worldwide have increased nearly eight inches over the past hundred years; Earth's atmosphere has warmed by 1.5 degrees Fahrenheit since the year 1900; and since 1979, the Arctic Sea ice has diminished by more than 30 percent, as the NSIDC reports.

Everywhere across the globe, animal populations are being wiped off the face of the Earth at an alarming rate.

According to the World Wildlife Federation (WWF), we are currently in our Sixth Mass Extinction, losing up to 200 species a day. Entire economies and nations are experiencing multiple wildfires, hurricanes, heat waves, droughts, floods, and other extreme weather events we have never seen before during our lifetimes. Vital eco-systems are disappearing from our very eyes, and some have already utterly collapsed.

I have personally lived through multiple hurricanes. I was conceived during Hurricane Frances (2004), I was a newborn living without power through Hurricane Wilma (2005), my Christening was postponed due to Hurricane Katrina (2005), I calmed my New York neighbors' panic during Hurricane Sandy (2012), I saw my grandmother's home destroyed by Hurricane Irma (2017), and my mother's homeland decimated by Hurricane Maria (2017). I have witnessed, firsthand, the frantic preparation and chaos of watching adults debate whether or not they should lose wages and evac-uate a potentially life-threatening storm. Even the near misses such as Hurricane Dorian (2019), which at one point was a Category 5 nightmare aiming straight for our home located a few hundred yards from the beach, causes psychological damage not easily dismissed by the "myth" of climate change.

The numbers are solid, and the facts are in. The exces-sive burning of fossil fuels such as coal, natural gas, and oil are emitting gases that create a greenhouse effect—

where more sunlight passes through Earth's atmosphere than is absorbed or reflected—hence causing ground-level temperatures to rise. And Earth's warming is not due to changes in the position of the sun, as scientific observation since 1978 has closely noted.

In fact, a staggering 97 percent of climate scientists believe global warming is *man-made*. How do we know this to be true? Because the Earth became instantly cleaner as a result of the worldwide Coronavirus shutdown. Within the first four weeks, China's carbon dioxide emissions dropped 25 percent, dolphins were spotted swimming in the canals of Venice, and the smog over Los Angeles all but disappeared. But as soon as the world opens back up, pollution will more than likely return to its former levels.

This is a worldwide threat to all of humanity, and it is warranted that all countries must acknowledge climate change as a global security threat. And one way the United States can combat this incoming catastrophe is by implementing a set of economic plans to transition the United States into using more renewable energy, as well as using techniques to achieve proper resource efficiency. When history looks back at this time period to evaluate the presidential administrations of Donald Trump and whoever comes after him, we will be judged by our actions concerning this issue alone.

Several politicians have proposed different plans to achieve this. For example, the original sponsors of

the Green New Deal, Representative Alexandria Oca-
sio-Cortez and Senator Edward Markey, proposed an
FDR-like plan that includes transforming the United
States' energy system to one hundred percent renewable energy (creating nearly 20 million new jobs in the
process), rejoining the Paris Climate Accord, and providing $200 billion to the Green Climate Fund. Tom
Steyer, a progressive billionaire activist who was also
a 2020 Democratic Presidential Candidate, announced
that he would declare a climate emergency on day one
of his presidency, yet failed to win even one delegate
in the primaries.

How is it, with the level of technological innovation
our businesses have shown thus far, that we are still
digging things from the earth and placing them into
mechanical contraptions that have worked nearly the
same way for over a century?

*Everything we need to invent in order to survive exists
right now!*

Solar panels, electric cars, water-based engines,
wind-powered turbines, ocean cleaners, air cleaners,
solar glass, plant-based plastics, smart grids, carbon
cleaners, etc. The list goes on and on.

We all know why we refuse as a country to move to
renewable-based energy sources. It's the same reason
why we deny there's a climate problem to begin with.
Once again, we have built an entire economy based on
an immoral principle (of putting our personal needs

before that of the planet), and to eradicate it would cause short-term economic loss for powerful companies who back our current political figures.

It's as simple as that.

So, like our approach with healthcare, we must quickly but carefully transition the American economy into renewable-based energy, and hold a no-nonsense governmental stance against big business fighting this change.

What if every coal miner, fracker, and oil worker union came together and refused to work? What if they demanded a three-year severance package to switch careers? Free college? Free relocation? What would we do as a country?

We would switch to renewable energy as fast as humanly possible, that's what we would do.

And the world we live in today is on the verge of extinction if we do not take the necessary steps to combat this generation-defining crisis within the next eight years.

If you have children, and they are sitting next to you, look at them. Look at them closely. If you are a parent, I assume you want to comfort them when ill or injured, and provide the best care possible. You cook them the best foods your budget will allow. You send them to the best schools your budget will allow. You establish order and provide for your children the best disciplinary standards you possibly can.

Now, let me ask you a very plain question: If you want the best for your children, why would you ever oppose enacting efforts to salvage our planet from mass environmental destruction? If you want to give your children a healthy life, you must give them a healthy Earth. And this is why implementing The Green New Deal—or something similar—is not only common sense, it's imperative.

Most Americans share this mindset, but few take action to support change. In 2018, a Gallup poll found that 74 percent of Americans are in favor of stronger environmental laws, but rarely do environmentally strong candidates make the top of the list. It is time for every American, across the political and societal spectrum, to raise their voices and demand solid solutions to an ever-increasing global threat that will inevitably lead to our doom.

The best news is that science has already given us a clear, indisputable road map to recovery. The IPCC and Paris Agreement have outlined all of the necessary steps we must take as a global entity to reverse the damage: reduce CO_2 emissions by at least 50 percent, limit the global temperature rise below 1.5 degrees Celsius, dramatically slow down the use of carbon dioxide in our CO_2 budget to give us more time to reverse the damage, and practice equity where wealthier countries get down to zero emissions faster so that smaller countries have time to catch up.

According to *The New York Times*, "the United States—with its love of big cars, big houses, and blasting air-conditioners—has contributed more than any other country to the atmospheric carbon dioxide that is scorching the planet. That means we are the biggest polluters in history, and we walked away from the Paris Climate Deal."

In sum, this must change immediately, or I am afraid every other point I make in this book will be moot.

CHAPTER 6

Education

MARK KANTROWITZ OF the *Wall Street Journal* reports that between the years 1993-2015, the average student loan debt in each year's graduating class has risen from less than $10,000 to $35,000. Senator Sanders, in his book *Our Revolution,* describes that nearly 7 out of 10 students graduating with a bachelor's degree will leave school with some amount of debt, with the average graduate exceeding $50,000 in student loans. In his book *Debt Free Degree,* Anthony O'Neal states that number is closer to $35,000 for students attending public institutions.

The fact is, 45 million young people are now shackled with nearly $1.6 trillion in student loan debt across the country, and it's not getting better. This statistic alone is shameful on the part of the wealthiest nation in the world.

College has become more and more expensive over the last few decades. According to my sources, tuition and fees at a public, four-year university in the present time costs more than $10,000 annually. That number skyrockets even higher when accounting for room and board expenses, reaching a shocking $21,000.

Thirty years ago, that number was just $3,360 when adjusted for inflation.

What puzzles me is why so many people would have agreed to take on so much student debt?

Isn't it obvious that the rising cost of a college education was meant to filter out the lower socioeconomic classes from being qualified enough to take high-paying jobs away from the privileged class? Why haven't we made this societal injustice part of the national discussion?

Yes, money is a filter. It's why certain gyms charge $500 a month while comparable machines can be found at gyms charging $10 a month. It's why country clubs exist and charge $25,000 annual golf memberships. It's why some private schools charge $45,000 a year for a first-grade education. It's not because their gym, golf course, or school is truly that much different in terms of amenities warranting such a drastic difference in pricing; the higher costs are simply there to ensure a certain level of clientele, nothing more.

This is the beauty and freedom of America in that people can charge as much as they like for their products and services as long as they do not have a monopoly on it or are the sole providers of a critically necessary item or service (like cars, insulin, or kidney dialysis).

So, why would a young person agree to take on $100,000 worth of college debt knowing his or her profession's starting salary would be less than $40,000 a year? According to the website, MagnifyMoney.com, a $100,000 loan at a 6.8 percent APR equates to monthly payments of $1,151 for ten years. That's an enormous amount of money for a single person to pay for ten years! Rent, groceries, insurance, car payments, all leave very little left on a monthly basis.

———

IN ADDITION, THE student loan debt crisis has been exasperated by states slashing funding for higher education. For example, according to the American Council on Education, Colorado has cut spending for public higher education by nearly 70 percent between 1980 and 2011. Arizona and South Carolina have also cut funding by 62 percent and 66 percent, respectively, during this same time frame. Furthermore, the Center on Budget and Policy Priorities found that 48 states (with the exceptions of Alaska and North Dakota) are spending *less* per student than they did before the 2008

Recession. These funding gaps are negatively impacting students by forcing collegiate institutions to significantly raise the cost of tuition to make up the difference.

For this reason, more and more people are leaving college with back-breaking debt that will drag them down for practically the rest of their lives. Various sources indicate that nearly three million older Americans still have student loan debt and are relying on Social Security to help pay off some of what they owe. The Federal Reserve reports that the average student pays $393 a month, and even that is a large chunk of money when first starting out as a young person.

Some Americans are even incurring massive debt without a degree to earn enough to pay it back. Between fiscal years 2015 and 2016, *the U.S. News and World Report* found that 3.9 million undergraduates dropped out with federal student loan debt. Imagine trying to pay off $393 a month for ten years when your high-school graduate co-workers are making the same wage as you are.

In order to address this mounting economic crisis, many Progressive politicians have advocated using taxpayer dollars to make public collegiate institutions tuition-free. Some politicians, such as Vermont Senator Bernie Sanders, have even gone as far as to propose canceling all student loan debt for the nearly 45 million Americans who owe money. He was quoted as saying, "In a generation hard hit by the Wall Street crash of

2008, [my plan] forgives all student loan debt and ends the absurdity of sentencing an entire generation to a lifetime of debt for the 'crime' of getting a college education."

Student loan debt is such an economic burden that it has recently surpassed the outstanding sum of all credit card and car finance debt in the country, according to a recent article published in *The Economist* magazine.

The United States should have taxpayer-funded, public college education to ensure there is equal economic opportunity for all American citizens. Implementing such a program would spur economic growth, incentivize many more Americans to pursue a college degree, and help mitigate the barriers being imposed by the growing severity of income inequality.

Several conservative policymakers believe that a college education should *not* be publicly financed in the United States. They argue that spending billions of taxpayer dollars to subsidize tuition fees will actually do very little to help students avoid incurring a massive amount of debt, as there are many additional costs, including books, housing, food, transportation, insurance, and more.

However, the simple fact of the matter is that providing public, tuition-free college will help students reduce the amount of money they will owe when they fully join the economy as a life-long consumer of goods and services.

Without loans, the chance of obtaining a college degree is otherwise out of reach for many students. *The Harvard Business Review* found the rising costs of attending college is forcing many families to take out loans in order to pay for the various demanding expenses of enrolling in higher education. And according to an article written by the College Board, tuition accounts for nearly 40 percent of total average college costs. In addition, a CNBC article, titled "Here's How Much More Expensive It Is for You to Go to College Than It Was for Your Parents," found that between 1987 and 2017, public college costs have increased by 213 percent.

However, I think it is important to note that well-funded private educational institutions such as Georgetown, Harvard, Princeton, and Yale, offer robust financial aid packages for families that make less than $150,000 a year. On average, out-of-pocket costs to attend an Ivy League school in 2020 is around $28,000, and it can be as little as $10,000 a year according to *The U.S. News and World Report*. This is definitely a wonderful opportunity for students who qualify to attend these schools, as starting salaries after graduation also tend to be higher.

If the United States government wants to invest in future generations of Americans, it is absolutely critical that we provide taxpayer-funded, public college education to all eligible citizens who are willing to pursue a college degree. The wealthiest nation on the planet, by far, has more than enough economic resources to ensure that future generations have a shot at making it into the upper middle class and beyond. So, to address the concerns of conservatives who fear that allocating billions of dollars to subsidize tuition fees will not solve America's student loan debt problem, we must turn back a few pages in American history.

THE SERVICEMEN'S READJUSTMENT Act of 1944, more commonly known as the G.I. Bill, was a law signed by President Franklin D. Roosevelt that provided several economic benefits for returning World War II veterans. Under this law, 2.2 million veterans were able to earn a tuition-free college education, forty percent of whom would not have been able to enroll in college otherwise.

The Debs-Jones-Douglass Institute calculated that the G.I. Bill generated a staggering $35.6 billion over three and a half decades, and it added an extra $12.8 billion in tax revenue for the United States. The G.I. Bill provided taxpayer-funded college education to hundreds of thousands of successful dentists, engineers, doctors, scientists, accountants, teachers, attorneys, Supreme Court Justices, presidents, and so many more brilliant, generation-defining people.

Young Americans in 1944 put their debt-free college education to good use. They bought homes, automobiles, started families, and invested into the economy.

When right-wing politicians proclaim that spending billions of taxpayer dollars to publicly fund college education will only bring the nation toward the path of financial insolvency, remember that tuition-free college is the reason why the United States of America is an economic superpower next to none. What we did for military veterans in the 1940s and the economic benefits that followed, can most certainly be translated into present times. People who earned a burden-free college education would utilize it and invest into the economy.

Study after study shows there is no greater societal investment than college education, per an academic essay written by Max Page and Dan Clawson of the National Education Association. It is therefore appropriate to make the conclusion that implementing a taxpayer-funded public college education will help mitigate the crushing burden felt by millions of Americans all across the nation by spurring dynamic economic growth.

As per their report, "Macroeconomic Effects of Student Debt Cancellation," the Levy Economics Institute stated: "There is mounting evidence that the escalation of student debt in the United States is an impediment to both household financial stability and aggregate consumption and investment. The increasing demand for college credentials coupled with rising costs of attendance have led more students than ever before to take on student loans, with higher average balances. This debt burden reduces household disposable income and consumption and investment opportunities, with spillover effects across the economy."

With such a debilitating burden as the collective $1.6 trillion of outstanding student loan debt owed by millions of aspiring students across the country, we must put partisanship aside and make higher education more affordable for all Americans.

If countries such as France, Norway, Finland, Germany, and Sweden can offer a free or low-cost college education to its citizens, then the United States—who has a much larger economy than the aforementioned countries—can most certainly do so as well. If we are to mobilize our national economy, provide equal opportunity for aspiring young people, and invest in future generations, then it is most critical that we provide tuition-free, public college education to all those who deserve it.

So, how do we pay for it?

There are many possibilities. We can cut military spending in low-risk countries. We can move capital gains taxes from a separate category of 20 percent to regular income tax brackets. We can implement a three percent national sales tax. We can increase the corporate-tax rate from 21 percent to 30 percent. We can reduce the amount of time profitable companies can write-off their losses. We can raise property taxes by one percent.

There are literally a thousand ways we can pay for this. And unlike every other politician in office, I am not afraid to say that I absolutely embrace taxes. Smart taxes. Painless taxes. The kind that cell phone companies charge on our bills and we never even notice. It's how we tithe as a country. It's how we raise money to fix things that truly matter. And once we realize that paying higher taxes is a *privilege* much like driving a fancier car—an act of gratitude for having succeeded in a Capitalist society where not everyone gets an equal start—only then will we be able to provide a lifestyle for all Americans that truly feels special.

While I am in favor of tuition-free, public two-year and four-year college education for eligible American citizens, I am *not* in favor of completely canceling all student loan debt. Former New York City Mayor Michael Bloomberg has proposed canceling all student loan debt incurred at predatory or for-profit colleges and universities. While I do agree with Bloomberg on this particular issue, I simply believe that canceling all student loan debt will lead to a slippery slope of demands from the American public.

If we are to pay the $1.6 trillion of college debt, then what about paying off medical debt?

Students knew what they were getting into when they signed their loan applications. The terms were spelled out for them. However, people who incur medical debt did so without their full consent. An uninsured man who is rushed to the hospital for a heart attack did not have an opportunity to evaluate the APR and monthly payment terms before finding himself going home three days later with a six-figure noose around his neck.

Instead, I believe the United States should adopt a more pragmatic and incremental approach to this issue akin to what former Vice President Joe Biden and Michael Bloomberg have proposed in the 2020 Democratic Presidential Race. According to *The Economist*, both Biden and Bloomberg would reduce the student loan debt repayments from 10 percent of income to 5 percent. Joe Biden has proposed all debt-forgiveness tax free and raising the repayment threshold to $25,000. Michael Bloomberg, as I have previously mentioned, stated that he would forgive all student loan debt unethically incurred at predatory or failed for-profit universities, and impose an exemption of debt forgiveness up to $57,000 from tax.

That, to me, sounds fair.

EVEN LEADERS OF the past supported free education. Our 19th Republican President, Rutherford B. Hayes, believed that education was the launchpad to prosperity, and for political and economic participation to be shared among all members of society, he supported the establishment of universal accessible public education in the United States.

I strongly believe all Americans need to live by this model.

Now, the problems we face in this country extends beyond higher education. It is imperative we recognize the United States of America is no longer the best in the world when it comes to educating our young folks. In the year 2000, we were ranked 18th in the world in mathematics. In 2015, we fell to number 40, meaning within the span of 15 years, we fell 22 ranking positions. Furthermore, we slipped from 14th in the world in science to a mediocre 25th, and dropped from 15th to 24th in the world in reading.

As a young man, this greatly concerns me.

Between the years 2004-2005, as reported by Sean Carroll in the article, "Nationalize Public Schools," in the United States, the poorest counties on average spent less than $7,500 per pupil, while the wealthiest counties spent more than $17,500 on each student.

Now, I think it is completely unacceptable that a Mississippi seventh-grader learns something different than a seventh-grader in New York. Put it this way: You hired two builders to build a house. You want both to do a good job. Obviously, you would want the both of them to have new, strong equipment to accomplish the task.

No one would want to have one worker have outdated, rusty tools, and the other one to have reliable ones.

So why are we doing that with our youth?

Although the nationalization of schools is a direct contradiction to the Tenth Amendment—specifically the notion that states retain the authority to exercise any power that is not delegated to the federal government as long as the Constitution doesn't expressly prohibit it—this is where the idea of states' rights over centralized government fails horribly. Various localized governments, having to rely on local property taxes alone to maintain public schools, gives way to an inherent inequality that creates a disadvantage for many Americans.

If the value of a home in one state is $75,000 and that same exact house is valued in another state for $750,000, how can we expect their school systems to be comparable?

This is why we need to nationalize our public education system and give the federal government the power to establish and maintain all public schools. We can no longer finance education through state and local revenue; we must rely on our central government to provide such services, the same way we rely on the federal government to provide Social Security and allocation of money to the Armed Forces.

And for those readers who feel much antipathy towards centralized education, look at China, a country of over 1.3 billion people. China's state-sponsored system of public education is run by the Ministry of Education. And how is China doing? The *New York Times* reported in 2010 that China surpassed Finland as *first* in the world in math, reading, and science PISA rankings in the year 2009. If China can do it, the United States most certainly can as well.

I have spoken to several public-school teachers who oppose the nationalization of our primary and secondary education systems, and they argue that demographics, language barriers, and immigration issues make local entities better suited to create curricula that help unique populations thrive.

I couldn't disagree with this philosophy more. Although I recognize certain groups require additional services, such as learning English or reading support, these classes should and must be in addition to a core curriculum taught at all schools at the same time.

I, myself, having fully recovered from Autism, know how challenging this can be. I attended a special school in Florida for Autistic children at the age of three. Then, after attending two full years, was moved into a mainstream kindergarten class, failed miserably, then moved to New York City, where I was forced to repeat mainstream kindergarten a second time at P.S. 6 on the Upper East Side.

The entire time I was in school, I was receiving speech therapy, occupational therapy, headphone therapy to cure my Apraxia, and behavioral therapy outside of my traditional classes, all while learning the same subjects as my mainstream peers. And although it took me years to catch up with my classmates, I was able to, because Manhattan public schools are no joke. They take their role of preparing leaders of the future very seriously.

Under Mayor Bloomberg's administration, 22 out of 25 of the best schools in the state were located in New York City. By the time I returned to Florida, I was completely prepared, and I have been excelling in the highest-level classes ever since.

Naturally, I am extremely fortunate to have an iron-willed mother who insisted on removing gluten and casein from my diet, fed me liquid fish oil by the buckets, gave me liquid vitamins that turned my teeth yellow, and subjected me to every holistic treatment available at the time. I stopped flapping my arms, rolling my eyes backward, and spoke my very first sentences around the age of four, but *I can assure you that I remember every single thing that happened around me before that.*

I may have looked like I was "out of it," but I was one hundred percent conscious and aware. Which is why it is important we should not exclude lessons for learning-disabled children or those who are learning English for the first time. Naturally, children should be placed at different levels within a grade that best suits their abilities, but children learning basic math in Idaho, should be learning the same thing as children in basic math in New Jersey. Colorado teens in Honors English should be learning the same things as teens in Honors English in Maine, and so on.

And like our healthcare system, despite our poor rankings, we still exceed the OECD average for spending per student! Once again, we are spending more money per capita than a lot of other countries on public education, yet we fail to rank the best.

I will not accept mediocrity when it comes to education. We currently have the resources to make our public-school system rank in the top five countries in the world in every single category. I will not accept anything less for my future children, and neither should you.

If we survive the climate crisis, then education needs to be a top-priority issue. The only way we can truly make America great again is by strengthening our base and making our youth more innovative, resourceful, and resilient than any generation before it.

CHAPTER 7

Labor, Welfare, and Wages

BEFORE THE CORONAVIRUS pandemic, the United States economy was doing extremely well. The stock market was flourishing. The DOW and S&P 500 had reached all-time highs. The national unemployment rate was at a record low. Even stagnant wages had been up slightly. More importantly, our 45th president, Donald J. Trump, took credit for every single bit of it, and roughly half of America wholeheartedly agreed with him.

As many economists would agree, there is a major flaw with praising *any* current president for the success of an economy. Most presidents inherit the rebounding or declining economic seeds planted in the administration before him or her. And in this case, President

Trump inherited a rebounding economy when he was elected, and it was President Obama who actually produced the great economic results that Trump enjoyed for the first three years of his administration.

Under President Barack Obama, who served from 2009-2017, the United States unemployment rate dropped from ten percent in 2010 at the height of the 2008 Recession to less than five percent right around the General Election of 2016. Factcheck.org discovers that, under Obama's administration:

- The economy gained a net 11.6 million jobs
- The S&P 500 stock market index rose 166 percent
- Wind and solar power energy increased 369 percent
- The number of people without health insurance dropped by 15 million

Data from the U.S. Bureau of Economic Analysis shows the annual average growth for the 2019 fiscal year was 2.3 percent. This pales in comparison to the 5.5 percent peak achieved in the second quarter of 2014, under Obama's administration. Furthermore, if we go all the way back to the 1950s and 1960s, the GDP of our nation was valued much higher than today.

Of course, the economy under Obama wasn't perfect. And yes, many people complained about certain economic conditions under him (including a lot of my family members). But there is no denying the underlying evidence that suggests President Trump inherited his economic success from his predecessor.

In economics, inflation can be described as an overall increase in prices in the market economy, thereby causing the purchasing value of money to decrease. *The Guardian*/CNBC reported that the average cost of living for an American family of four is between $58,900 and $148,400, depending upon geographic location.

Yet despite this, roughly 50 percent of U.S. workers earn less than $38,000 per year. And the inflation rate in 2019 was 2.3 percent YOY. It's clear these numbers do not add up to a comfortable lifestyle for the majority of Americans.

While we do not currently have hyperinflation—like Venezuela is experiencing—our pre-pandemic situation did include prices going up, contributing to the financial misery affecting many Americans today. And one measure of counteracting this problem is raising the federal minimum wage to $15.00 per hour, and requiring at least 75 percent of all positions within a company give 40 hours a week to every employee, as companies are reducing the number of full-time employees to get out of federal guidelines to provide benefits.

For example, according to Reuters in 2018, 50 percent of Walmart's 1.5 million-person workforce based in the U.S. were part-time, up 20 percent from 2005. As America's largest employer, they only recently raised the minimum wage to $11.00 per hour. In addition, multiple studies show that a large percentage of those part-time employees need federal assistance, primarily food stamps and Medicaid. And given Walmart's net profit of $4.14 billion last year, the government should be charging Walmart directly for feeding its workers.

But we don't.

This is an example of how unchecked capitalism can destroy our country.

Last year, research showed that inflation was out-pacing the rate of wages earned by workers, causing the purchasing power of the American dollar to recede. The U.S. Department of Labor reported that between July 2015 and the most recent increase in the federal minimum wage, 8.1 percent of purchasing power of the American dollar was lost due to inflation.

Before our economy was frozen by the Coronavirus, things were getting more expensive, and most people were not making enough money to counteract it. According to David Autor, Alan Manning, and Christopher L. Smith in their report, "The Contribution of the Minimum Wage to U.S. Wage Inequality over Three Decades: A Reassessment," the United States has not raised its federal minimum wage since 2009, and failure to do so has accounted for 48 percent of the increase in inequality between workers at the middle and bottom of the wage distribution since 1979.

As the issue of income inequality engulfs our contemporary economy, we must guarantee ordinary Americans a decent, living wage. This is more important than ever as we rebuild our economy to offset the damage of shutting the world down for months to avoid a microscopic killer, or so we believed.

In addition to issuing temporary emergency checks to all Americans under the CARES Act (Coronavirus Aid, Relief, and Economic Security Act of 2020), the government must permanently raise the federal minimum wage, so that low-wage workers can survive this economic tsunami and endure the pressure of this uncertain U.S. economy.

As a country of wealth and opportunity, it is absolutely imperative we lift all people out of poverty.

———

IN 2014, A Congressional Budget Office (CBO) report found that merely raising the minimum wage to $10.10 an hour from the current $7.25 would salvage about 900,000 people from the depths of financial misery. And the Economic Policy Institute found that $22.1 billion would be injected into our economy if the former scenario was implemented.

Imagine the benefits if we raised the minimum wage to $15.00 an hour!

This would rekindle the spirit of the working-class. This would inject more consumer dollars into the economy. This would allow average people the ability to save more money for emergency funds. And let me assure you, businesses will not suffer if we raise the bar in regard to how much an employer must pay their worker, because everyone would have more money to spend and thus more money to produce.

What conservative-leaning thinkers overlook is that raising the minimum wage for all workers would reduce government welfare spending. Low-income workers will not have to rely on government-run financial assistance programs to compensate their inadequate, starvation-level salaries.

In 2014, The Center for American Progress found that raising the federal minimum wage to $10.10 would diminish government spending on the Supplemental Nutrition Assistance Program (SNAP) by roughly $4.6 billion. For clarification, the Department of Agriculture-run SNAP program provides food-purchasing assistance and benefits for low-income and no-income people. Citing the Economic Policy Institute in 2016, nearly $7.6 billion would be shaved off from annual government spending on income-support programs if the minimum wage was raised to $10.10. According to the same report, nearly two million Americans would no longer be dependent on government assistance programs if the aforementioned measures were taken.

Again, imagine the benefits if that number was $15.00 an hour.

———————

AT THE TIME of this writing, more than 40 million people have filed for unemployment benefits, and we still have no idea the extent of the long-term damage the Coronavirus pandemic will have on our economy.

According to Ben Casselman of *The New York Times*, the national unemployment rate for April 2020 was 14.7 percent—by far the worst since the Great Depression. Two months earlier, the rate was 3.5 percent, a 50-year low. According to Jeff Cox of CNBC, the *real* unemployment rate, which includes workers not looking for jobs and the underemployed, surged to 22.8 percent—and we still have no idea if we have reached rock bottom yet.

What we do know, however, is that the lower income earners and working middle class will be hit the hardest, with entire professions, like restaurant servers, realtors, massage therapists, personal trainers, hairstylists, babysitters, dog groomers, tattoo artists, flight attendants, event caterers, actors, filmmakers, lifeguards, janitors, make-up artists—and so many more—completely out of work at the same time.

New unemployment claims will continue for months, if not years. State unemployment websites will continue to crash. Applications will continue to be lost. People who remain employed will continue to live in fear that they will be next. The entire system is in chaos, all because of a government mandate to stay home and avoid getting infected by something that will probably be ubiquitous in a decade.

Inevitably, more people than ever will end up on welfare for the first time. And the intricate political subject of welfare with the presence of programs such as Social Security, Medicaid, Medicare, and various other financial-support initiatives such as SNAP, will, in my estimation, no longer have the connotation it once had before the pandemic.

According to the United States Census Bureau, the official poverty rate in 2018 was 11.8 percent. In addition, before the pandemic, 38.1 million people lived below the poverty line, and although this is an improvement compared to previous years, it is still an unacceptable number.

Digging deeper, the U.C. Berkeley Labor Center found last year that over half of fast-food workers relied on at least one poverty assistance program, and the United States spends roughly $152.8 billion each year on welfare programs to support low-income families.

That's right. Before Coronavirus, a large percentage of families receiving welfare had at least one family member working 40 hours a week. Isn't it shameful to have an economic system where a person with a steady, reliable, full-time job cannot meet their own basic needs?

In 2018, the total cost of welfare programs summed up to one trillion dollars when counting annual federal and state fiscal budgets. In a country where a CEO can make more per second than what his or her workers earn in a month, I'm sure we can give a helping hand to modest, hardworking Americans, and maintain adequate welfare programs for families who desperately need it.

In the United States of America, our economy is structured columns encrypted under the sink-or-swim system. There are many people who are unable to lift themselves out of the abyss of financial deprivation without outside intervention. Government is established by the people to protect the natural rights of all its participants, and thus obliged to advance the common good for everyone within that particular communal jurisdiction. The preamble of the United States Constitution includes a provision to "promote the general Welfare" of the entire country.

I truly believe that we, as a nation, owe a responsibility to all citizens to provide a basic social net to those who are not able to enjoy the comforts of our free enterprise system.

In 2020 and beyond, the faces of welfare will drastically change.

It will no longer be "those" people living on the wrong side of the tracks. Now, the person receiving welfare will be your neighbor, your coworker, your barber, your dogwalker, your personal trainer. Now, the need for a helping hand is greater than ever.

Even with businesses struggling to return full-force, if we raise the federal minimum wage, families across America can relieve themselves of the anxiety of putting food on their tables, and once again believe they might have the opportunity to live the American Dream.

Clinton, who bombed Kosovo, all
ional Declaration of War.

Resolution of 1973, which limited
ority to commit American Troops to
thout the approval of Congress, has
y nearly every administration since.
r strengthen this resolution before we
foreign threat, particularly those who
within our borders.

t to note the Department of Homeland
he an outstanding job at thwarting ter-
American soil since 9/11, and although
to guarantee or expect they catch and
gle one, it is an impressive record of six
ents resulting in 82 deaths over 20 years,
he 227 domestic mass shootings that killed
over the last ten years.

ary spending goes far beyond supporting
g tanks, and designing new missiles. It now
s border security which has been a red-hot
e last five years.

ig to NPR, President Trump's signature cam-
mise—the proposed Mexico-United States
all—has already diverted $3.8 billion from
rtment of Defense budget. This is in addition
1 billion that's already been identified to con-
ore than 500 miles of new barrier fences along
border with Mexico.

CHAPTER 8

Military, Defense, and Border Security

THE UNITED STATES of America, by far, spends more
on military might than any other country in the world.
In fact, according to the Peter G. Peterson Foundation,
the U.S. spends more money on the military than the
next seven countries combined.

The U.S. Department of Defense budget for 2020
was $718 billion, which, according to the Brookings
Institute, comprises 15 percent of all federal government spending and 3.2 percent of GDP. This is significantly more than the world's second and third largest
military budgets: China, who spends $181 billion, and
Saudi Arabia, who spends $78.4 billion. Even with its
larger size, Russia shockingly comes in at number six,
only spending $61.6 billion a year on its military, despite

having influence over so many other countries in strategic operations.

I believe the United States should maintain a strong and well-funded military. In fact, my family is part of the millions of Americans who rely on the Department of Defense budget, as my dad is retired U.S. Navy, and has received a monthly pension since the age of 38.

Although I think it's critical we continue supporting our troops and their families in every way, I do feel there is room to strengthen international cooperation, end costly wars in the Middle East, and streamline expenses to further solidify our reputation and position in the world.

John Anderson—who ran in 1980 as an independent candidate against Ronald Reagan and Jimmy Carter—once argued that it is impossible to cut taxes, increase military spending, and balance the budget all at once. And although I find this to be true, I believe the need for national security outweighs the need for a balanced budget, although it should certainly be our goal to reconcile the two within the next five to ten years.

The truth is, given our advancements in technology, traditional face-to-face war is an outdated means of resolving conflict, and national security spending should shift more toward cybersecurity. According to Farhad Manjoo of *The New York Times*, "Technology is turning armed conflict into an endeavor increasingly dominated by what war scholars call 'asymmetric warfare,' meaning

---

tha
stren
migh
superp

Nee
the past
to contro
Freedom,
sibly as po

Accordin,
which my da
dollars, thous
the Taliban lik
involvement in
lion dollars, and
of Mass Destruct
today.

and President Bill (
without a Congress
The War Powers
the president's auth
armed conflicts w
been challenged l
We need to furthe
face yet another
wish to harm us
It is importan
Security has do
rorist plots on
it is impossible
stop every sin
terrorist incid
compared to t
1,297 people
Our milit
bases, buyin
also include
topic for th
Accordi
paign pro
Border W
the Depa
to the $1
struct m
the U.S.

IN ADDITION, IT is
power of Congress to
1, Section 8 of the Un
Executive Branch has slc
It was first violated in re
Truman, who sent troops
Kennedy, who sent troop

So, where did this new funding come from?

Again, according to NPR, it takes $1.5 billion originally allocated for buying equipment for National Guard and Reserve units, such as trucks, generators, and spare parts, as well as fighter jets and ships. But no matter who pays for it, the mere existence of this expensive, ineffective project is what troubles me most.

Wikipedia states that the total length of the continental border is 1,954 miles. And researchers at both Texas Tech University and Texas A&M University suggest that a wall would be ineffective at the border. Why? Because the Department of Homeland Security reports that most illegal immigration isn't coming from the Mexican border, but rather from overstaying visas and using the Visa Waiver Program.

When Fox News host Chris Wallace questioned former White House Press Secretary Sarah Huckabee Sanders about the flow of terrorists coming in at the southern border on January 6, 2019, Mr. Wallace referenced the State Department, as they found no credible evidence that can be cited to suggest any suspected terrorist was ever found at the southern border. Wallace argued that nearly 4,000 suspected terrorists were caught at airports and other travel systems, but not one of them was caught at the Mexico-United States border.

ThoughtCo.com has stated that President Trump's primary motive in building the wall is to prevent losing nearly $113 billion in lost income tax revenue. But the White House Office of Management and Budget suggested in a letter to Congress that only 814 miles needed barrier fencing, which would mean that over 1,100 miles of the Mexican-American border would still be barrier-free.

Now, I doubt people intent on coming unlawfully into this country would be deterred by this proposed incomplete wall. Desperate people seeking entry would find a roundabout way to arrive on American soil. I am sure a border wall would have been effective during ancient times, yet, we must acknowledge we live in the present, and that people can travel various ways other than by foot or by land.

Furthermore, there are various environmental studies to suggest that erecting a border wall would negatively impact the wildlife of either side, disturbing animal migration patterns and damaging the habitat of a whole host of organisms.

The answer is not barriers or walls; it is common sense, benevolence, and comprehensive immigration reform. We must no longer throw children in cages and separate families in detainment. In fact, the issue of immigration is so large that I will address it in its entirety in a future book, but for now, we must stop the circulation of hatred toward undocumented people, and hold integrity to ensure that everyone who seeks the American Dream can achieve it.

Dumping our money, manpower, and natural resources into a useless barrier that will do nothing but deplete the military of necessary funding, should cease immediately.

CHAPTER 9

Universal Basic Income

ENTREPRENEUR, PHILANTHROPIST, ATTORNEY, author, CNN contributor, and former 2020 Democratic Presidential Candidate, Andrew Yang, sent shock waves—and giggles—through the nation with his campaign promise of a *Freedom Dividend* to all citizens.

According to Yang, the proliferation of automation would kill so many jobs that only a steady government check would keep the economy stable. Under his plan, every single American over the age of 18 would be provided with $1,000 a month indefinitely, no strings attached.

Most of America—including many Democrats—laughed at the idea, considered it a ridiculous attempt at instituting socialism, claimed Republicans would never allow it, and so on. As a result, on February 11, 2020, Andrew Yang dropped out of the presidential race with 0.45 percent of the popular vote and zero delegates.

Exactly one month later, on March 11, 2020, Republican President Donald Trump told the American public that he would be sending every person a check for "$1,000 or more" on a quarterly basis, as part of a trillion-dollar stimulus package designed to combat the drastic economic downturn caused by COVID-19.

And just like that—a $1,000 monthly check program that sounded absolutely preposterous—immediately became the most widely accepted idea on social media within *days*. And although the final amount decided by Congress was actually $1,200 per person for individuals earning $75,000 or less, $2,400 per couple earning $150,000 or less, and $500 per child—how ironic is this turn of public sentiment?

While I respect Andrew Yang as a bold innovator and appreciate his forward thinking, I do not believe implementing a permanent Universal Basic Income (UBI) in the United States will mitigate the effects of income inequality, spark economic growth, or even help people get by in this highly disparate economy.

Why? Because the fundamental problem with implementing a UBI program is that it will raise the cost of everything at the same time.

Much like a high tide raises all boats, a $12,000 annual income boost for all citizens will allow people to easily and instantly spend more for desired items, and retailers and manufacturers will adjust their prices accordingly. The cost of consumer goods will go higher. Rents will increase. Food will increase. And not many people will even notice, until they find themselves once again with the same bottom line purchasing power as before.

In addition, a UBI significantly de-incentivizes an entire class of individuals from working or producing goods and services. What nineteen-year-old living at home will feel compelled to get a job? Charles Wyplosz, Professor of International Economics at the Graduate Institute at Geneva, Switzerland, stated in part "...if we pay people, unconditionally, to do nothing...they will do nothing," and this will create a less productive economy.

While the idea of a UBI is popular among Silicon Valley magnates, such as Elon Musk and Mark Zuckerberg, for the exact same reason Andrew Yang cites—and I sincerely value the opinions of all three men—I cannot see how it will alleviate the poor and middle classes.

Mr. Yang's former presidential website claimed that, "putting money into people's hands and keeping it there would be a perpetual boost and support to job growth and the economy," and states "[the implementation of a UBI] would enable all Americans to pay their bills, educate themselves, start businesses, be more creative, stay healthy, relocate for work, spend time with their children, take care of loved ones, and have a real stake in the future."

While the intentions behind a Freedom Dividend is respectable—and the results of which are something that both the Democratic and Republican Parties should aim for— the implementation of such a program is highly impractical.

The New York Post reported in 2018 that the financial investment firm Bridgewater Associates calculated that granting every American citizen $12,000 a year will cost $3.8 trillion annually. The same report found the cost of a UBI program will equate to 78 percent of all taxes collected for social programs, or nearly one-fifth of the nation's entire annual economic production. While there are multiple estimates made by several economically focused organizations, the message is clear: a universal basic income of $1,000 a month to every American citizen—no strings attached—will serve as an unsustainable financial burden to the taxpayer base. It will take away important tax revenue needed to revamp healthcare, combat climate change, and support education.

On the other hand, in 2017, the Roosevelt Institute found that the implementation of a UBI program would generate 4.6 million jobs and consistently grow the economy by 12 percent. Proponents of a Freedom Dividend argue that providing $1,000 a month to every American would serve as a great incentive for people to find employment, invest in entrepreneurial activities, and engage in creative projects that will spark profound cultural innovation that will benefit generations to come.

Other countries have already shown us that providing guaranteed money to unqualified citizens does very little to spark job creation. For example, Finland enacted a two-year government experiment from January 2017-December 2018, that provided nearly 2,000 random Finns the equivalent of $635 a month, or $7,620 a year. A 2019 online article published by *The New York Times* reported that—while those who received the monthly check did become happier—this initiative did not contribute to job creation whatsoever. According to the article, Ohto Kanniainen, the chief economist for the trial, stated the results were not surprising, as many jobless people in the experiment had few skills or regularly struggled with difficult life situations. Miska Simanainen, one of the top researchers behind the Finnish experiment, said that while some individuals did find work, their chances to secure employment were no higher than a control group of people who weren't given any money, as reported by BBC News.

In analyzing the results of the Finnish experiment, the Organization for Economic Cooperation and Development (OECD), stated that implementing a UBI initiative nationally in Finland would cause significant income redistribution without eliminating poverty in the country.

Robert Greenstein, President of the Center for Budget and Policy Priorities (CBPP), stated in an online article that: "If you take the dollars targeted on people in the bottom fifth or two-fifths of the population and convert them to universal payments to people all the way up the income scale, you're redistributing income upward. That would increase poverty and inequality rather than reduce them."

In addition, various studies show that a UBI won't help combat addiction, poor health, financial illiteracy, and many other factors that contribute to poverty. A UBI program is inherently flawed because people will be allowed to irresponsibly waste their money on alcohol, gambling, sex, drugs, energy drinks, vaping, and other activities that promote self-destruction or societal dysfunction.

However, several major studies show that people are indeed initially "happier" when they are granted an appropriated check every month from the government. But the lasting effects of long-term, fulfilling employment clearly outweigh any short-term pleasure a new UBI program would deliver.

———————

IN CONCLUSION, I do not believe that a UBI is what the United States needs at this moment. We have already spent ten percent of our GDP in funding the first round of CARES Act payments in response to COVID-19, and that was one payment of $1,200 for every individual who qualified. The cost of providing $1,000 to every American citizen *every month* will cost the taxpayer base nearly $40 trillion over the next decade. Additionally, countries such as Finland essentially disproved the claim that implementing a UBI would spark economic productivity, and multiple studies written by academic scholars suggest the Freedom Dividend will actually increase poverty and income inequality in the United States rather than reduce it.

Let me be clear. All of these studies were conducted before the Great Pandemic of 2020. The truth is, I may change my mind on this issue in the immediate future. If unemployment reaches 30 percent or more, or if poverty hits all-time record highs, I may seriously reconsider my position on this issue. I have tremendous respect for the leaders in Silicon Valley, and if they see this as a solution to future problems the rest of us cannot see, then I am open to the idea.

But if things return to normal within a year and Democrats want to provide equal economic opportunity for all citizens, then a UBI program is most certainly not the appropriate path to take.

CHAPTER 10

Capitalism and Entrepreneurship

IF THE MOST recent presidential elections have proven anything, it has shown us how much Americans love, cling to, and identify with the term *Capitalism*. As Merriam-Webster defines it, capitalism is an economic system characterized by private or corporate ownership of capital goods, by investments that are determined by private decision, and by prices, production, and the distribution of goods that are determined mainly by competition in a free market.

I define it as a free-enterprise system in which people voluntarily offer goods and services for the exchange of wealth.

And like many other things, capitalism has its benefits and drawbacks. The conservative side often praise our free-market system by constantly reminding us how ugly other government systems are, such as communism, authoritarianism, and their absolute favorite, socialism. Liberals, on the other hand, only like to highlight the dark side of capitalism, including homelessness, violence, and poverty. And although both are right, the beauty of capitalism is there for the taking, and I couldn't be more supportive of a free-market economy with several safety measures in place.

What kind of safety measures?

I think we should embrace a new kind of capitalism, where *optional* goods and services continue to thrive in a free-market system while the prices of "survival-necessary" goods and services are controlled by the government. For example, the price of televisions should remain free market, whereas the price of HIV medications should have limits. The price of luxury homes should remain free market, while the price of rentals should have national caps (similar to New York City's rent control laws). The prices of luxury items should continue to be free market, whereas the price of basic necessities should have national guidelines. I call this new approach "smart capitalism," and although some would argue that it sounds a lot like democratic socialism, I assure you my rebranding of the phrase would make the concept more palatable to the millions of struggling Americans who refuse to live in anything but a capitalist society.

In fact, many economists believe that income inequality in this country is the highest it has been in 50 years. CEOs of Fortune 500 companies earn nearly 400-500 times more than their employees at the bottom of the hierarchical ladder. The Council of Economic Advisers at the White House issued a report finding there are half a million people—that's 500,000 men, women, and children—who comprise the homeless population. From coast to coast, you can visibly find hundreds of economically powerless people who have succumbed to the most impoverished life that our capitalistic system allows for: eating dinner out of garbage cans, begging people for money to buy a can of Pepsi, and being completely ignored by most of society.

My mother taught me many things as a young child. One of her most powerful speeches was that capitalism means we live in a sink-or-swim economy, and the consequence of having limitless opportunity to succeed was that there is no real safety net for those who don't make it. As I mentioned before, she also believed that it was easier to "just *be* the one percent" through hard work, rather than trying to change the rules, and that there are only ten paths to wealth in America, including the ritualistic saving of a modest income (power of compounding interest), starting your own company, inheriting it, marrying it, inventing it, investing it, creating it, manufacturing it, selling it, or winning it through the lottery.

This speech, in particular, stuck with me. And although my mother is quite weird given her profession of writing horror books and movies for a living, I think she was close to being right.

Capitalism forces economically disadvantaged people to formulate how they are going to outsmart those with wealth in order to survive, as outlined by Friedrich Nietzsche in *On the Genealogy of Morality*. In this book, he outlines how the "master morality" values pride and power, while the "slave morality" values kindness, empathy, and sympathy. The master judges actions as good or bad, whereas the slave judges actions by religious or evil intentions. Over time, the slave class becomes smarter, having to constantly outwit the master class in order to survive, and over centuries, becomes the ruling class.

This, to me, sounds very similar to the top and bottom socioeconomic classes in capitalism, but for whatever reason, I do not see the type of evolution that Nietzsche describes in the bottom tiers, for I feel the upper tiers have somehow found a way to subdue it.

Despite all this, however, capitalism is still the *best* economic system that has ever appeared on the face of the earth. I have witnessed homeless people collecting aluminum cans to earn five dollars to eat. I have witnessed multi-millionaires spontaneously donating $250,000 of their hard-earned money for a charitable organization aimed at ending human sex trafficking (more on this later). I have been in rooms full of wealthy celebrities, and in rooms full of people struggling to make ends meet, as the same system that freely allows people to become billionaires also plunges millions into economic disparity of which they cannot climb out of.

Yet, somehow, capitalism has produced an array of products that serve both the rich and poor. The photographic film, electric light bulbs, condensed milk, cotton candy, airplanes, frozen food, microwaves, GPS, traffic lights, and so many more things that are used by people of all races, religions, sexes, and nationalities around the world, were invented by brilliant American inventors. And to me, that is a beautiful thing.

While capitalists should pay taxes to benefit the rest of society, many people who amass considerable fortunes do donate their money to various causes for good. America is the leading philanthropic country in the world, donating as much as $427.71 billion to U.S. charities in 2018 alone, according to Giving USA.

What Democrats often forget is that the people we criticize most, actually help support the causes we care most about.

For example, Amazon CEO, Jeff Bezos—who has a net worth of nearly $150 billion according to Forbes—recently committed ten billion dollars of his own personal wealth to fight climate change through the creation of the *Bezos Earth Fund*. This fund will help cover the costs of scientists, activists, and NGOs looking to "preserve and protect the natural world." Also, in 2018, Bezos and his partner gave two billion dollars to fund nonprofit schools and homeless charities through their *Day One Fund*. Michael Bloomberg of Bloomberg L.P. cofounded Mayors Against Illegal Guns and launched the Everytown for Gun Safety organization, which is considered the largest grassroots force for gun safety with nearly six million supporters. The philanthropic donations of Facebook CEO Mark Zuckerberg and his wife, Priscilla Chan, totaled nearly $214 million in 2018. Bill Gates and his wife, Melinda, have distributed more than 50 billion dollars' worth of grant donations through the Bill and Melinda Gates Foundation. Motivational speaker Tony Robbins and his wife, Sage, have contributed millions of dollars and more than half a billion meals to feed hungry families across America and around the world.

I can keep going on and on about the noble philanthropic efforts that several millionaires and billionaires have invested their wealth in. However, I believe my point is clear: we *need* wealthy people. We cannot alienate those who are the backbone of the American economy, including the working middle class and the top one percent. Yes, we need to police Wall Street and Silicon Valley. Yes, we need to raise taxes on those who earn the most money in this country. Yes, we need to impose common sense regulations on businesses so that their economic activities do not conflict with the rights of everyday citizens.

But when progressives chant "abolish billionaires!" Republican strategists are secretly clinking champagne glasses together, as they know America will never vote for such a thing. At least, not in this current climate, where even the poor are afraid to vote for a democratic socialist presidential candidate.

Instead, we need to realize that multi-millionaires and billionaires utilizing their financial resources to help boost noble efforts is not a bad thing. And while we most certainly need to mitigate the harmful effects of income inequality in this country, it is important to remember that all the goods that you use, all the produce and food that you consume, and even the book or digital reading device you are holding in your hands at this very moment, could not have been cultivated, financed, or manufactured without people investing their time and effort into the companies producing them.

That's not trickle-down economics. That's simply common sense.

———————

ANOTHER IMPORTANT ISSUE that should be discussed is how we should support small businesses and young entrepreneurs. In 2016, the Census Bureau's Annual Survey of Entrepreneurs found that employer firms with fewer than 500 workers employed approximately 46.8 percent of private sector payrolls. Employer firms with fewer than 20 workers, on the other hand, comprised 16.8 percent of private sector payrolls. Furthermore, the nation's nearly 30 million small businesses generated over half of the U.S. GDP in 2014, according to the Small Business Administration.

This is a personal issue for me, as my paternal grandfather is a proud small business owner of a family-run property management firm based in West Palm Beach, Florida. And from my experience, I understand that we need to incentivize citizens, who likely don't have as much wealth as Jeff Bezos or Warren Buffett, to invest their time and financial resources into small business ventures.

Frankly, the Trump administration has been fairly popular among small business owners. A Wilmington Trust survey of 1,000 privately held businesses, conducted between May 24 and June 14, 2019, found that 59 percent of respondents either "strongly or somewhat support" the current administration's approach to economic stability.

However, more can be done to spark economic growth in the small business sector.

For instance, the Associated Press found that between 2007 and the first half of 2019, applications to form businesses that would likely hire workers fell by 16 percent. Furthermore, racial minorities are also severely underrepresented and discriminated against in this particular sector of American commerce. Researchers found in a 2018 UC Berkeley Public Law Research Paper that minority borrowers are frequently charged nearly 5.6 to 8.6 basis points higher interest on mortgage refinance loans, which are calculated to result in disparities of $250 million to $550 million on an annual basis (for clarification, one basis point is equivalent to 0.01 percent change; a one percent change is equivalent to 100 basis points).

What this study essentially says is that racial minorities who are looking to start a small business are commonly discriminated against when applying for loans. To that point, the National Community Reinvestment Coalition found in 2019 that there were steep declines in government-backed lending to African-American business owners between 2008 and 2016. It is also worth noting that a 2018 U.S. Small Business Administration report found that business ownership is significantly lower among natural-born Latino men and women than non-Latino white men and women. The disparity in business income among U.S.-born Latinos is also very concerning.

For these reasons, I think the government should take the following steps that Michael Bloomberg once proposed in order to foster competition in the marketplace:

- Repeal government loopholes that allow giant, multi-national corporations to immunize themselves from market competition as well as laws that give them special advantages over smaller competitors

- Provide funds for cities and towns to either create or strengthen entrepreneurship centers in their respective jurisdictions

- Increase the federal budget for the Small Business Investment Company program, which was created by Congress in the 1950s, that licenses private providers of financial resources and encourages subsidized financing that helps incentivize small business growth

- Allocate those funds to underserved and economically disadvantaged communities

- Establish a nationally funded corps of business-driven mentors who will help aspiring entrepreneurs succeed

- Double the value of contracts going to minority-owned small businesses and promote the certification of government contracts to qualified businesses run by underrepresented groups of people

- Increase training and supervision over banks in order to reduce racial discrimination in the small business loan industry and combat the predatory practice of redlining

In conclusion, our capitalist society is the most wonderful ground for people, ideas, and entrepreneurial seeds to grow. There are simple measures our government can take to soften the downside of our sink-or-swim economy in order to create a more pleasurable and positive experience for everyone in America.

Smart capitalism should be our next step. I hope to foster this concept from this point forward and help implement the safeguards that will ensure our position as a compassionate world leader for centuries to come.

CHAPTER 11

Abortion

ON MARCH 22, 1972, the Equal Rights Amendment (ERA) passed the Senate and House of Representatives with tremendous bi-partisan support and was eagerly sent to the states for ratification. Since the Constitution requires a three-fourths majority to ratify any new amendment, Congress gave the states a total of ten years to ratify it, yet only 35 of the necessary 38 states met the ratification deadline after conservative-leaning opponents claimed it would remove gender-specific protections including: exclusion from the war draft, the ability to collect alimony in case of divorce, and preferred caregiver status in child custody disputes.

The ERA has been reintroduced nearly every session of Congress since 1982 and continues to be ignored by the states who refuse to ratify it. For the life of me, I was perplexed as to why our modern society would be so calcitrant to ratify such a simple statement of inalienable rights. Women are *clearly* equal. Women deserve to be paid exactly the same as men. Women have the same choices in life as men do—and in some cases even more—as the modern female has the choice to serve in the military, pursue a professional career, be a stay-at-home mother, or do all three within her lifetime.

So, I had to know, what were the scary *52 words* that almost changed America nearly forty years ago? Here they are:

Section 1: Equality of rights under the law shall not be denied or abridged by the United States or by any state on account of sex.

Section 2: The Congress shall have the power to enforce, by appropriate legislation, the provisions of this article.

Section 3: This amendment shall take effect two years after the date of ratification.

What? That's it?

And then I researched further about the history of the ERA and found that another, more controversial right was being advocated by the ERA leaders of the day—Gloria Steinem, Betty Friedan, Bella Abzug, to name a few—and realized it had forever cast a shadow on the Amendment that should have been ratified without question.

And that issue was *abortion*.

―――――――――

RIGHT ABOUT NOW, many readers of this book have classified my belief system as progressive, perhaps even slightly leaning toward democratic socialism. And for those rooting for me to blindly advocate for the Left, I offer my apologies in advance, as I am about to take a 180-degree turn from the stereotype of a young, naïve, liberal snowflake.

As previously mentioned, I am *pro-human* from conception to grave. And there is no issue that I disagree with more than the practice of abortion.

Yes, I acknowledge I am only fourteen years old. Yes, I concede that I am male. Yes, I understand that abortion is a complex issue, with many difficult circumstances surrounding any unwanted pregnancy. Yes, I am aware this is an extremely contentious and emotionally charged subject that could jeopardize my political standing in the future. Yes, I graciously acknowledge that I do not fully understand what it is like to be a woman, nor do I plan to transition or become one, and I wholeheartedly respect *all* viewpoints on this highly controversial issue.

Yet, despite these important disclaimers, my conscience rejects me from aligning with the rest of the Democratic Party in supporting that a woman's reproductive rights trump an individual's right to life, or that the disposal of sacred, human life at any stage should be sanctioned by our government.

Our laws on this issue are hypocritical. If it is considered homicide under the Unborn Victims of Violence Act of 2004 to murder a pregnant woman's fetus, how can it be legal for this *same* fetus to be terminated by the mother? How can an individual's rights under the law be contingent upon the subjective condition of whether or not that individual's mother wants him or her to live? No other set of human rights is contingent upon the opinion of another individual in our country. So why would the *right to life* be subject to this notion?

There is no amount of evidence or argument that will sway my thinking into the direction that free, limitless, on-demand abortions should be legal in this country. The recent movement of women's rights advocates publicly bragging about the number of abortions they have had does little to further their arguments, as even many women who have had abortions would have preferred to seek alternatives had they been socially acceptable or available.

What we fail to realize in supporting a woman's right to decide is that half of the unborn children who are denied access into this world are *also* women who deserve the right to live.

Now, what we have failed to do as a government, is to provide the necessary tools to reduce the number of unwanted pregnancies to record-low levels. All contraception for both men and women should be free (paid for by the government) and widely available to anyone who wants it. Our single-payer healthcare system should cover all costs associated with pregnancy and delivery. Our society must remove the stigma of women who serve as surrogates or give up their babies for adoption, instead making them the heroes they truly are.

With that said, there are several difficult, complex circumstances that we must address when discussing this important issue:

1. If the mother's life is in danger medically

2. If the mother is a victim of rape

3. If the mother is below the age of consent (18 years old)

4. If the pregnancy is a result of underage incest

I will concede, the aforementioned circumstances make it very difficult for anyone to advocate a blanket ban on abortion, but we must drastically reduce those very specific case-by-case exceptions. For instance, I do not believe teenagers should be forced to give birth and raise children against their will. The U.S. Department of Health and Human Services found that teenagers who become mothers are more likely to drop out of school, develop mental disorders, and receive inadequate prenatal care.

In addition, multiple credible organizations such as the World Health Organization (WHO) have proven that mothers who are forced to be pregnant as rape or incest victims tend to suffer severe psychological damage during the process. And I think most people agree, even pro-life Americans, that abortion should remain an option when a mother's life is in jeopardy due to a medical emergency.

However, we must strengthen these exceptions. We should require a minimum of two doctors to agree in writing that a mother's life is in danger before a termination procedure can take place. We must prevent the increase of false rape reports by requiring women to show evidence of a police report being filed before a pregnancy was confirmed. The other exceptions—being of minority age and underage incest—are covered by a simple birth certificate showing the mother was under the age of eighteen when conception took place.

Which boils down to all other, on-demand abortions by women over the age of eighteen who knowingly participated in sexual intercourse with another consenting adult, should be abolished in its entirety in the United States. And I am not afraid to make this bold, controversial statement that may cast a shadow over my political career until the day I die, because I am indeed, a pro-life progressive.

From a legal standpoint, I am not afraid to stand up and say that I agree with the late Supreme Court Justice Antonin Scalia in the belief that *Roe v. Wade* is a flawed Supreme Court decision, based on a right to privacy found literally nowhere in the Constitution, and it must be overturned. The 1973 landmark case ruled that the Constitution provides "a guarantee of certain areas or zones of privacy," and that "This right of privacy... is broad enough to encompass a woman's decision whether or not to terminate her pregnancy." The Supreme Court also, however, declared that this right is not absolute, and it is the responsibility of state governments to ensure that the health of the mother is not in jeopardy during the procedure. In addition, the right to an abortion must be balanced against the interests of the state in protecting prenatal life.

What a load of nonsense. *Roe v. Wade* is one of the top ten worst Supreme Court decisions our country has ever made. In fact, the real "Jane Roe" in this landmark decision is by far the worst plaintiff in the history of the Supreme Court as she served as the poster child for the pro-choice movement in the 1970s, then accepted more than $450,000 to advocate for pro-life organizations in the 1990s, then reversed her decision again in a "death bed confession" documentary about how she conned us into thinking she cared about the issue at all.

That's right. Norma McCorvey—better known by her legal pseudonym Jane Roe—never even had an abortion. She gave birth to three daughters: one she gave away to her mother and two others she gave up for adoption. While married and pregnant with her third child in 1970, McCorvey agreed to serve as the plaintiff in this landmark case. She proudly stood on the steps of the Supreme Court in 1973 in celebration of its victory, then shocked her supporters in 1995 when she became a devout Roman Catholic and pro-life activist for two decades.

McCorvey admitted she felt that her participation in the case was "the biggest mistake of [her] life," according to her second memoir published in 1998, *Won by Love*. In addition, when she was the plaintiff in *Roe v. Wade*, she publicly said that the reason she was seeking an abortion was because she was raped. Later in life, however, she claimed that statement was a lie. Then finally, in the documentary *AKA Jane Roe* (filmed days before McCorvey's death in 2017), she reaffirmed her support for abortion and admitted: "It was all an act. I did it well too. I am a good actress."

Wow. What a train wreck. And we based one of our most important Supreme Court decisions on this wishy-washy plaintiff?

What better reason to repeal *Roe V. Wade* than to dismiss the original case based on the confession that the original motion was filed under the false pretense of rape.

IT IS IMPORTANT to note that I am not religious, nor do I even attend church at this time. I am, however, far from being an atheist. I am a strong believer in God. I believe in the Universe. I believe in Source. I believe this magnificent Energy creates all things. I believe in karma, synchronicity, visualization, and manifestation. I believe in the Law of Attraction. I believe in equal rights. I believe every woman deserves the same opportunities as men, the same wages, the same *everything*. It just so happens one gender was given this additional responsibility, and if men were biologically equipped with bringing new life into this world, I would advocate the exact same thing. And if I were sitting in front of the United States Senate being confirmed as a Supreme Court Justice, I would have no problem declaring my position, as I am today.

Several other legal intellectuals have heavily criticized the decision in addition to Justice Scalia. Then-Associate Justice William Rehnquist, in his dissenting opinion, declared that abortion "is not 'private' in the ordinary usage of that word. Nor is the 'privacy' that the Court finds here even a distant relative of the freedom from searches and seizures protected by the Fourth Amendment to the Constitution."

The Fourth Amendment explicitly states that: "The right of the people to be secure in their persons, houses, papers, and effects, against unreasonable searches and seizures, shall not be violated." Nowhere in the Constitution is the right to dispose of human life as a contraceptive method found. Furthermore, the Fourteenth Amendment declares that no state shall "deprive any person of life, liberty, or property, without due process of law; nor deny to any person within its jurisdiction the equal protection of the law." Because the federal Unborn Victims of Violence Act of 2004 protects fetuses and embryos from acts of mutilation and violence, the legal precedence of *Roe v. Wade* should therefore be considered unconstitutionally sound.

Several pro-choice advocates argue that the government should respect women's reproductive rights and legalize abortion to ensure that women have safe measures to it. That women will resort to dangerous "back-alley abortions" and die. Defenders of abortion hold the view that since nearly all abortions take place in the first trimester of the pregnancy—where the fetus is completely dependent on the mother as it is attached to the placenta and umbilical cord—fetuses are a part of the mother and cannot be regarded as a separate entity. Furthermore, they argue fetuses are not *people* and that mothers have the right to terminate their pregnancies at any time. And finally, they reason that adoption is not a legitimate alternative to abortion because very few mothers are willing to go through the psychological trauma of giving up their babies for adoption. After all, several statistical outlets show that less than three percent of white, unmarried women give their children up for adoption. That number is even lower for African-American women, standing at less than two percent.

However, I think it is appalling for Americans to support abortion as a method of contraception. A Guttmacher Institute article in 2018 discovered that 45 percent of all women having abortions had *at least one previous abortion*. In 2014, the Centers for Disease Control and Prevention calculated that 8.6 percent of abortions reported to them included women who had *three or more previous abortions*. If accurate, these statistics suggest that some women are relying on abortion as a last resort form of contraception.

Women do indeed have a right to control their own body. But the simple matter of fact is that a fetus is not *part* of the mother's body: it's a human temporarily living *inside* of a woman's body. It is a separate entity that has legal rights afforded to it. And if we have laws that prevent tenants from being evicted by landlords without due process, we must honor that small individuals have rights inside the womb as well.

Moreover, why should we bend the laws to protect women who seek illegal, back-alley abortions? Are we concerned with the health of drug dealers who seek backyard treatment of gunshot wounds? Are we concerned with the health of criminals who break their legs jumping over walls? Are we concerned with the health of cancer victims subjecting themselves to experimental treatments not sanctioned by the FDA? Why are we making the threat of back-alley abortions a reason to keep an inhumane practice *legal*? If a woman chooses to break the law and seek an unauthorized medical procedure, then that is her decision, and it should not impact the legality of the act whatsoever.

Another argument made by pro-choice groups is that middle class and wealthy women will always have the means of seeking abortions elsewhere, whereas the poor will not. Well, is it unfair for wealthy women to hop on a plane to avoid a court hearing while a poor woman must face her sentencing? This argument is utterly ridiculous. The wealthy will always have the choice to avoid the law, and to do so is their decision at their own peril. But to say it is *unfair* that rich women are able to circumvent an illegal practice, thus, we must make it legal so poor women are not forced to follow the law, is truly the lamest legal argument I have ever come across.

And while I understand that many Americans have very strong feelings toward this subject, I simply believe that abdicating the gift of motherhood just as a contraceptive method is inherently unethical in its entirety. No civilized society endorses the murder of several legally protected entities without serious ramifications. I personally view abortion as no different.

The indisputable fact is that unborn children are viewed as human beings by the United States government. Again, the federally passed Unborn Victims of Violence Act recognizes an embryo or fetus as a legal victim. The legislation states that it was enacted "to protect unborn children from assault and murder." It also includes a provision that declares an unborn child as a "member of the species homo sapiens."

And this is where Democrats have shown hypocrisy in their reasoning.

How do liberals and progressives have the conscience to be pro-choice while supporting stronger federal administration on firearms to prevent mass shootings? How do they call the caging of undocumented children inhumane while allowing thirty-year-old women the right to inject saline into 34-week-old, externally viable babies? How do they condemn the death penalty as an antiquated form of punishment, and denounce acts of war that send thousands of young men and women overseas to be unnecessarily slaughtered?

According to Valerie Richardson of *The Washington Times*: "Even most pro-choice Americans oppose late-term abortion, according to a newly released poll, putting them at odds with the Democratic push for state legislation removing barriers to third-trimester procedures. A survey conducted by You.gov with the pro-life group Americans United for Life found that 66 percent of U.S. adults who identify as pro-choice opposed third-trimester abortions, and 68 percent oppose abortions the day before a baby is born. As expected, the opposition was stronger among all adults surveyed: 79 percent rejected late-term abortion, and 80 percent opposed day-before-birth abortion."

Liberals must come to the realization that supporting policies that promote the deaths of nearly 862,000 unborn children each year in the United States alone (Guttmacher Institute, 2017) significantly undermines their message of being *pro-human*.

This is why Evangelicals are flocking to support President Trump and the Republican Party, because the Democratic Party represents the elimination of core family values that have defined traditional life here in America for so long. We must re-evaluate this stance. Core family values should be a concept shared by all parties. Families of all kinds must be included.

Of course, some adult mothers and fathers simply cannot raise their children in a clean, safe, and adequate environment for a variety of reasons. This is where the subject of adoption comes into play.

According to the National Council for Adoption, the percentage of infants given up for adoption has declined significantly from 9 percent to just 0.5 percent during the years of 1973 to 2014. At the same time, millions more of Americans—single, married, straight, and gay—are seeking to adopt children they know they can afford, love, and properly raise.

How is the increasing demand for children not increasing the supply? Because we have wrongfully stigmatized women who are brave enough to place their children up for adoption, and this must cease immediately.

Pro-choice advocates have rebutted this alternative by insisting that giving a child up for adoption is more emotionally damaging than terminating a pregnancy. But what about the emotional damage of women unable to conceive? Or the emotional damage of cancer survivors who were forced to choose between chemotherapy and motherhood? Which type of emotional damage wins?

I think it is important for struggling mothers to understand there are alternative options to assist them in providing the best possible experience for themselves and their fetus. And again, we must applaud them as heroes, and if we do institute a widespread change in reproductive rights, then it's in everyone's best interest to follow the law.

In summary, while I do recognize the indisputable fact that women have a right to control their body up to the point of conception, I do not think it is prudent for the Democratic Party (or society as a whole) to endorse the mass disposal of prenatal life while trying to preserve life through healthcare, welfare, gun control, and capital punishment.

The preservation of life is not a gray area; it is a natural right, guaranteed in writing by the Declaration of Independence, where all people have "the right to life, liberty, and the pursuit of happiness."

Yes, there are extreme circumstances in which abortion may be necessary. I am in favor of broad and early sex education, free birth control, better adoption policies, and the advancement of other pre-conception, contraceptive methods.

But take a moment and think of every person you personally know who was adopted at birth.

What if they never existed? What if *you* never existed?

Both Greta Thunberg and I were born with Autism Spectrum Disorder. On February 13, 2008, I scored a 37 on the Childhood Autism Rating Scale (CARS), which is one point away from being classified as "severely autistic." Greta Thunberg, on the other hand, was diagnosed with Asperger's Syndrome. Twelve years later, this book is being professionally published, and Greta Thunberg is the world's leading advocate for climate change.

Now, what if a test had existed in 2004-2005 showing our parents we would be born with Autism? Would we have both been terminated during pregnancy? If so, who would be out there advocating for Generation Z? What other leaders have we lost among the 862,000 souls that were denied entry last year?

Abortion is not only a moral issue; it is a legal one. And the contradictory laws of our country countering the preservation of human life versus the right to privacy will eventually be reconciled...

And life will win.

CHAPTER 12

Gun Violence

FROM COLUMBINE TO Parkland, Sandy Hook to Santa Fe, and Las Vegas to Blacksburg, an identical theme has emerged: gun violence continues to jeopardize the lives of thousands of Americans of all races, ages, and ethnicities.

Every day, loving parents who lost a child in a school shooting must wake up to the horrific realization that they will never again be able to hug them goodbye as they board the school bus. They will never be able to witness them become respectable young men and women. They will never be able to cradle the grandchildren that are no longer possible.

Life will never be the same.

VALENTINE'S DAY WAS the second-year anniversary of the morning Nikolas Cruz murdered 17 people at Marjory Stoneman Douglas High School in Parkland, Florida. This now-infamous high school is located only one hour south from where I currently live and is the alma mater of three of my extended family members.

Nikolas Cruz was a mentally disturbed nineteen-year-old who legally purchased a semiautomatic AR-15-style rifle under Florida statute. While then-Governor Rick Scott took some action and signed legislation to tighten firearm regulations, including raising the minimum age to buy a gun from 18 to 21, imposing longer waiting periods, and establishing more barriers to prevent mentally ill citizens from purchasing firearms, the issue of gun violence throughout the United States remains a limp issue. Here are the facts:

- According to the Giffords Law Center, nearly 36,000 Americans are killed by guns each year—that's an average of one hundred deaths per day.

- From 2014 to 2017, the number of gun deaths increased by 16 percent nationwide.

- The CDC found that over 1.2 million Americans have been shot in the past decade.

- The CDC also reported that, of the nearly 36,000 Americans who are killed by guns each year, over one-third are gun homicides.

- The nonprofit Gun Violence Archive reported that 417 mass shootings occurred in the United States in 2019. Essentially, there were more mass shootings *than days in the year*. This statistic is based on the criteria that at least four people were shot per event.

- Associate professor Adam Lankford of the University of Alabama found that between 1996 and 2012, while the United States only comprised of five percent of the global population, a whopping 31 percent of the world's mass shooters were American.

- Due to the Coronavirus shutdown, March 2020 was the first March since 2002 without a school shooting.

Two years after Parkland, major federal gun control legislation has still not been enacted. Two years after Parkland, many Americans have just accepted gun violence as a way of life. Two years after Parkland—and despite 135 new state laws to address gun violence—a mass shooter still has the capacity to murder nine people in 30 seconds with an AR-15-style weapon, which is exactly what occurred in Dayton, Ohio, last year.

Many young Americans, such as Parkland graduate and gun control activist David Hogg, have taken their anger with the inefficiency of the American political system to the streets after the Parkland shooting. Many politicians respond on social media by sending their "thoughts and prayers" to the families of the victims affected by deadly mass shootings.

I'll say this as politely—yet directly—as possible: Generation Z will no longer accept your "thoughts and prayers." The youth of this country will not accept the status quo, and once we reach voting age, we will vote out every person in Congress who blocks federal gun control laws to keep firearms out of the hands of the mentally challenged and dangerous criminals.

I should mention here that I fully support the right of all qualified American citizens to keep and bear arms, as granted by the Second Amendment of the United States Constitution. The amendment reads: "A well-regulated Militia, being necessary to the security of a free State, the right of the people to keep and bear Arms, shall not be infringed."

The landmark Supreme Court Case *District of Columbia v. Heller* (2008) declared that the Second Amendment guarantees an individual's right to own a firearm for self-defense, hunting, and other traditionally lawful purposes. Justice Antonin Scalia, writing for the majority of the Court, declared in his opinion: "We find that they guarantee the individual right to possess and carry weapons in case of confrontation. There seems to us no doubt, on the basis of both text and history, that the Second Amendment conferred an individual right to keep and bear arms."

Justice Scalia went on to declare, however, that the right to own firearms was not absolute, comparable to Freedom of Speech protected by the First Amendment. He continued: "Nothing in our opinion should be taken to cast doubt on longstanding prohibitions on the possession of firearms by felons and the mentally ill, or laws forbidding the carrying of firearms in sensitive places such as schools and government buildings, or laws imposing conditions and qualifications on the commercial sale of firearms ...We think that limitation [the precedent established by the 1939 Supreme Court Case *Miller v. United States* that the types of weapons constitutionally protected were those 'in common use at the time'] is fairly supported by the historical tradition of prohibiting the carrying of 'dangerous and unusual weapons.'"

The dissenting members of the Court, comprised of Justices John Paul Stevens, Ruth Bader Ginsburg, David Souter, and Stephen Breyer, argued the Second Amendment was established only to protect Americans' rights to possess firearms for military purposes. In his dissenting opinion, Mr. John Paul Stevens wrote: "The Second Amendment was adopted to protect the right of the people of each of the several States to maintain a well-regulated militia. It was a response to concerns raised during the ratification of the Constitution that the power of Congress to disarm the state militias and create a national standing army posed an intolerable threat to the sovereignty of the several states...the view of the Amendment we took in Miller—that it protects the right to keep and bear arms for certain military purposes, but that it does not curtail the Legislature's power to regulate the nonmilitary use and ownership of weapons—is both the most natural reading of the Amendment's text and the interpretation most faithful to the history of its adoption."

Justice Scalia, to rebut this legal argument, explained the former clause of a "well-regulated militia" did not void the latter phrase of "the right of the people to keep and bear arms." He wrote: "The Second Amendment is naturally divided into two parts: its prefatory clause and its operative clause. The former does not limit the latter grammatically, but rather announces a purpose...although this structure of the Second Amendment is unique in our Constitution, other legal documents of the founding era, particularly individual-rights provisions of state constitutions, commonly included a prefatory statement of purpose...nowhere else in the Constitution does a 'right' attributed to 'the people' refer to anything other than an individual right...'[t]he people', refers to all members of the political community, not an unspecified subset..."

Many people on the Left—such as progressive radio talk show host, pundit, and political commentator Thom Hartmann—have proposed repealing the Second Amendment in its entirety. Taking the provided legal precedence into account in the Court's ruling in *District of Columbia v. Heller*, I vehemently oppose the repealing of the Second Amendment as I believe public backlash would be so intense that it could even trigger a Second Civil War.

Yet, evidence shows that most Americans are still extremely fed up with the level of gun violence that is occurring in all corners of the nation. An *Economist/ YouGov* poll conducted in February 2018, found that nearly one in five American voters either "somewhat" or "strongly support" repealing the Second Amendment. According to the poll, 39 percent of Democrats agree with the previously described statement; 16 percent of independent voters; and only 8 percent of Republican voters. Furthermore, the poll found that almost half of American voters either strongly or somewhat support the modification of the Second Amendment to include provisions that would permit stricter gun control regulations. Of the total sampled group, 76 percent of Democrats said yes, modify the Second Amendment; 38 percent of Independent voters; and 26 percent of Republican voters.

After every mass shooting, lawmakers frequently raise the idea of imposing universal background checks on all firearm transactions, from gun store purchases, private sales, and gun shows. After all, a Gallup Poll conducted in 2017 found that a whopping 96 percent of Americans are in favor of more universal background checks.

Yet, while this may seem like a reasonable solution to help combat the gun epidemic plaguing our nation, sadly, it isn't.

INSTEAD, I PROPOSE a combination of free mental healthcare and substance abuse treatment services to all through a single-payer healthcare system, a national phone hotline to anonymously report anyone making threats to harm others through the use of guns, coupled with a national ban of assault weapons, a nationally sponsored gun buy-back program, and a universal gun-licensing system that would effectively keep the majority of firearms out of the hands of potential criminals while also allowing law-abiding citizens to exercise their right to bear arms.

So why no universal background checks? There are two major reasons why:

1. When implemented, they are ineffective in reducing gun deaths, as they do nothing to measure *intent to do harm.*

2. The FBI's database is missing millions of records.

Researchers at John Hopkins University studied how the implementation of expanded background checks in 1991 was "not associated with changes in firearm suicide or homicide" in California, according to their findings. The 1991 law required a comprehensive background check (CBC) for all gun purchases, with a few exceptions, and barred anyone who was convicted of a misdemeanor within the past decade from obtaining a firearm. They found that over the ensuing decade after the law's implementation, net change in the firearm homicide rate was not affected whatsoever by the law.

In addition to being ineffective in reducing firearm-related deaths, the Federal Bureau of Investigation (FBI) is actually missing millions of records from their database. According to *The Washington Post*, the Charleston church shooter, who detestably murdered nine African-American followers of Christ as they peacefully studied the Holy Scripture together in 2015, was able to pass his background check, despite having a record.

According to *The Guardian* in 2017, it was discovered that the Sutherland Springs church shooter also passed his comprehensive background check before murdering 25 people (and an unborn child) with an AR-15-style semi-automatic weapon. The Texas shooter had a history of domestic abuse, though the United States Air Force failed to provide legal documents to keep him from obtaining a firearm.

As explained by a 2019 video produced by Vox, it takes an average of 108 seconds to get a response from the FBI's National Instant Criminal Background Check System. That means a person with a criminal history or record of mental illness, is able to legally obtain a weapon within two minutes and go on about his or her day. And while background checks may screen out some dangerous people from acquiring guns, the fact is that the United States Federal Government must implement a licensing system that will screen out not only the most dangerous Americans with proven criminal records, but also prevent *potentially* dangerous people who have not been convicted of crimes in the past from purchasing a weapon.

According to the Giffords Law Center, twelve states—Massachusetts, Nebraska, Iowa, Illinois, Michigan, Hawaii, New York, New Jersey, Connecticut, Rhode Island, North Carolina, Maryland, and the District of Columbia—have already implemented a licensing system for future gun owners in their jurisdictions.

For illustration, here are the steps to purchase a gun in Massachusetts:

1. The applicant must first take a gun safety course.

2. Then he or she must submit a permit application at a police department.

3. Then he or she must provide contact references and fingerprints for a thorough background check.

4. Not only is the FBI database searched, but all local law enforcement agencies located anywhere they have ever lived are directly contacted. Fur-

thermore, the Department of Mental Health is
also contacted to ensure the person doesn't have
a serious history of mental disturbance.

This lengthy process, which takes a minimum of three
weeks to complete, is a much more thorough and comprehensive checking system that ensures only mental-
ly-stable, law-abiding citizens are able to buy a gun.
The Massachusetts Executive Office of Public Safety
and Security reports that nearly 97 percent of people
pass these rigorous standards.

According to John Hopkins Bloomberg School of
Public Health, when Connecticut implemented their
firearm licensing law in 1995, the legislation was found
to be associated with a 40 percent drop in gun homicides. Since then, gun suicides have also decreased by
15 percent.

Missouri, on the other hand, enacted a licensing
system for decades before they repealed it in 2007.
Since then, gun suicides have increased by nearly 16
percent, while the change was also credited with a 17
to 27 percent increase in the gun homicide rate.

Extensive research suggests that a universal licensing
system will be efficient in preventing the majority of dangerous and mentally ill people from acquiring weapons,
while also ensuring that good people are able to purchase guns for self-defense and recreational purposes.

With all various sources of information being provided, I still feel like it is important to acknowledge the issue of whether we should reimpose an assault weapons ban, similar to what the United States did with the Federal Assault Weapons Ban (AWB) in 1994.

As I have personally come into contact with several AR-15-style weapons, I can confidently proclaim that the United States should reimpose an assault weapons ban.

Some Democratic politicians, such as California Congressmen Eric Swalwell, have proposed banning the civilian use of military-style semiautomatic weapons and then buying weapons back from those who are willing to comply with the law. Under this plan, anyone who disobeys the prohibition will be criminally prosecuted.

Semiautomatic assault weapons were created for the military and other law enforcement agencies. While this may upset many, in no way should civilians be able to legally obtain such weapons of carnage. Even if a law-abiding, good faith citizen wants to purchase such a firearm, it should be illegal for them to do so. They should even be banned in shooting ranges and hunting clubs, for there is no reason for anyone outside the Department of Defense to even learn how to use one.

Some conservatives may argue that a ban-and-buy-back plan would be ineffective in reducing gun violence. After all, according to an article published by the Statista Research Department, assault rifles aren't even the most preferred choice of weapon for mass shooters. Here are the facts:

- In the United States, from 1982 to 2019, handguns were used 142 times in 94 incidents
- Rifles were used 55 times in 47 incidents
- Shotguns were used 30 times in 26 incidents

As you can see, most active shooters use more than one weapon per shooting. However, this statistic is flawed. What it doesn't tell you is that the AWB was enacted from 1994 to 2004, so naturally, these statistics are skewed. The reality is that a federal prohibition on all semiautomatic weapons and high-capacity magazines will significantly reduce the type of gun violence in America that continues to terrorize our people.

ANOTHER ISSUE CONTRIBUTING to the severity of our gun epidemic is Congress's shocking protection of a for-profit industry that directly results in the deaths of tens of thousands of Americans every year: *the gun manufacturers.*

Passed by Congress and signed by President George W. Bush in 2005, The Protection of Lawful Commerce in Arms Act (PLCAA) prohibits "qualified civil liability actions" against gun manufacturers and dealers in court. Essentially, this law protects the gun industry from nearly all civil lawsuits brought against them.

Of course, there are a few exceptions to this law. And while the Act does allow people to sue manufacturers for "product defects," the simple truth is that the PLCAA is an absurd law that grants broad legal immunity to the gun industry.

You see, no other industry has ever been granted this high-level of legal protection, not even pharmaceutical companies or food enterprises.

So, why does this matter?

According to Grand View Research, if the tobacco industry was provided with the same amount of congressional immunization as the gun manufacturing industry, they would still be selling their cancer-causing products to teenagers. Just think, the global tobacco market is expected to reach nearly $695 billion by 2021, despite the hundreds of billions of dollars they have already paid out in class-action settlements and wrongful death lawsuits. Imagine what their global market cap would have been if Congress would have made tobacco lawsuits illegal!

Seriously, why does Congress allow lawsuits against products that gradually kill people over time, but indemnifies something capable of killing ten innocent children in less than 30 seconds?

On any day of the week, people lose loved ones to cancer, heart disease, and diabetes—conditions all caused by products we consume on a daily basis. And if Congress is even one bit concerned with maintaining quality of life for every American, then we have to equate America's gun problems with our overall health crisis.

This would require us to repeal the PLCAA as soon as possible.

Now, some gun advocates argue that congressional immunity is needed to protect the Second Amendment. Frankly, this is a ridiculous argument. As I have previously stated, the Supreme Court's interpretation of the Second Amendment is not a license to kill. And if we were to adhere to this line of reasoning, then Congress would need to pass legislation making it unlawful to file libel and defamation of character lawsuits because the First Amendment protects freedom of speech.

Again, this make no sense. Therefore, the PLCAA must be repealed immediately.

WHILE IT IS true the Small Arms Survey found in 2017 that there are more guns than people in the United States, the number of Americans who own firearms only comprise a small portion of the population.

In 2016, Harvard University found that 78 percent of Americans *don't even own a gun.* An unpublished Harvard/Northeastern survey obtained by *The Guardian* a few years ago also discovered that just *three percent* of the American adult population own half of the guns in the United States!

This means that somewhere between 3 and 22 percent of Americans own at least one firearm. The rest of us—anywhere between 97 and 88 percent of America—are tolerating mass shootings of children in support of the Second Amendment.

So, how do other countries handle this issue?

In April 1996, eighty-eight people were shot in Port Arthur, Tasmania, by a man who possessed a Colt AR-15 and L1A1 SLR battle rifle. This indescribable act of human carnage directly caused the deaths of 35 people.

What did the Australian government do to ensure that no event like this ever happened again? They passed the National Firearms Agreement that, among other things, banned all semiautomatic rifles from civilian use. How has the NFA law affected gun violence in Australia—a country of 25 million people—since the law was passed?

In 2016, the University of Sydney, in a study published in the *Journal of the American Medical Association*, found that Australia hadn't experienced any major mass shootings (based on the criteria that five or more people were murdered) since the 1996 massacre. In May 2018, however, an Australian family of seven were found dead with severe gunshot wounds. This was the first mass shooting in Australia in the

over 22 years since their government banned semiautomatic weapons from commercial use! For 22 years,
Australian mothers and fathers could peacefully tra-
verse the streets of their nation without worrying that
a crazed perpetrator would slaughter them in the day-
light of their city.

My mother, who has PTSD from growing up in a
severely haunted house, walks around public places
like a soldier on patrol, looking for potential threats in
corners every day. She has no peace. This is how any vig-
ilant mother in America walks with her children today.

How many more lives will the United States let perish
before we act? How many more six-year-old bodies
must we zip up in bags before we have the courage to
stand up to the National Rifle Association (NRA) and
get semiautomatic assault weapons out of our society?

Why haven't the brilliant minds of Silicon Valley
invented new weapons of protection that use technology to sense aggression, read chemical imbalances in
the body, or shut down when touched by criminal fingerprints? If you can invent a driverless car that knows
the difference between a running dog and a coffee cup
in the road, surely you can invent a gun that knows the
difference between an angry bear, a threatening intruder,
and a crying child, *can't you*?

Time and time again, assault weapons are used in one
mass shooting after another. The shootings of Parkland,
Las Vegas, Orlando, Newtown, and Sutherland Springs,

among other places, all involved perpetrators with military-style assault weapons in their grasp. This doesn't even highlight that the average kill rate was nearly ten people every 30 seconds.

Let me repeat that. Ten people every thirty seconds.

For those who oppose banning all semiautomatic weapons, my message is clear: you are endangering the lives of thousands of Americans every single year by not agreeing to get these weapons off our streets.

Australia has proven to the rest of the world that banning all semiautomatic assault weapons from civilian usage *does* prevent mentally disturbed people from obtaining weapons of human destruction. The cause for the ban-then-buy-back program for assault weapons is a moral one, the goal of which is to protect the most fundamental right of any human being:

The right to life.

———————

IN CONCLUSION, IT is time for our government to stand up to gun violence. It is an embarrassment to the world when our lawmakers do nothing more than pretend to care via social media when a teenager takes out 17 innocent lives.

While there has been some progress in the fight against gun violence, such as the United States Department of Justice banning bump stocks in December 2018, mass shootings are still a problem in virtually every town, city, and county of America. Guns killing nearly 36,000 people a year is the equivalent of one 9/11 terrorist attack every single month on American soil.

The Second Amendment of the Constitution, as ratified in 1791, permits us to prohibit extremely dangerous weapons of carnage from civilian use. I believe it is essential that the United States provide free mental healthcare and substance abuse treatment services to all through a single-payer healthcare system, institute a national phone hotline to anonymously report anyone making threats to harm others through the use of guns, encourage new technologies to protect citizens, prohibit all semiautomatic weapons from commercial sale, and implement a federal licensing system that will screen out the most dangerous people from obtaining firearms.

It is time that we unite under one flag and stand together in combating this generation-defining issue that continues to affect every American in all corners of the country.

CHAPTER 13

Child Sex Trafficking

ACCORDING TO THE National Center for Missing and Exploited Children, roughly 2,000 children are reported missing each day in the United States. Most victims are abducted by people the child knows, but for the ones who are not, an unspeakable life of hell, and possibly death, awaits them.

In 2016, former President Barack Obama passionately and accurately summarized the horrors of human sex trafficking when he said: "I'm talking about the injustice—the outrage of human trafficking—which must be called by its true name: modern slavery. It is barbaric and it is evil, and it has no place in a civilized world."

Yes, children as young as toddlers are being sold abroad as sex slaves. Girls as young as five are working seven days a week in brothels. Pre-teens are being kid-napped and murdered for their organs. For instance, a ten-year-old boy can be bought in most countries for as little as $10,000, forced to service five men a day for several years, and when his body becomes too damaged, his heart can be sold on the black market for $250,000 for an organ transplant.

I wish I were describing some sort of disgusting horror movie, but I am not.

While older generations have a hard time compre-hending, let alone discussing, the subject of child sex trafficking, the truth is that my generation is who these monsters are after. Therefore, we must lead the fight and be the ones to end it.

Every single day, children across the world are praying to God that they be rescued from the darkness. And while human trafficking is indeed illegal in the United States, and the government has been trying to curb the amount of people being unethically exploited for decades, we still face an unprecedented number of inno-cent lives who have been forced to succumb to the evil abyss that continues to ruin hundreds of thousands of children every year. Here are the facts:

- According to the U.S. Department of Health and Human Services, more than 300,000 young people in the United States are considered "at risk" of sexual exploitation every year.

- The U.S. State Department has discovered, of the 600,000 to 800,000 people who are unwillingly trafficked across international borders every year, half are children and 80 percent are female.

- The U.S. State Department also found that between 14,500 and 17,500 people are trafficked into the United States annually.

- The U.S. Labor Department found that 148 goods that were identified from 75 countries were explicitly produced by forced child labor.

- Finally, the International Labour Organization calculated the number of modern-day slaves has reach a total of nearly 40.3 million people.

These children are often kidnapped on American soil, or while your family is on vacation, and you never hear about it on the news because no one wants to stare this level of evil in the face. While you should worry about the well-being of your children regarding the threats of human trafficking (especially since we live in a time of robust technological innovation that allows for the easy manipulation of young people), there is still something you can do to help eradicate the existence of the modern international sex trafficking industry.

If you were skimming through the pages of this book and contemplating whether or not to purchase it, (I appreciate it if you do), I would like to inform you that I will be donating a percentage of my net book royalties to the organization known as Operation Underground Railroad, or O.U.R.

I learned of this amazing organization when I attended Tony Robbins's 60th birthday party in Los Angeles, California, earlier this year, despite my mother having been a previous donor.

Founded by Timothy Ballard in 2013, Operation Underground Railroad is comprised of former CIA agents, U.S. Special Operations Forces members, and other support volunteers, who *physically rescue innocent children* from sex trafficking operations all around the world.

Tim Ballard served 12 years as a U.S. Special Agent for the Department of Homeland Security, on the Internet Crimes Against Children Task Force, and the U.S. Child Sex Tourism Jump Team. He helped infiltrate and dismantle dozens of trafficking organizations that kidnapped children and forced them into the sex slave industry. However, as a U.S. agent, Ballard was not authorized to rescue children if their cases crossed the border, or if the case could not be tried in a U.S. court. For this reason, he left his position and founded Operation Underground Railroad instead.

In the past six years of existence, O.U.R. has rescued 3,300 victims and assisted in the arrests of more than 1,800 traffickers around the world. The international law enforcement partners they train and empower have collectively helped rescue the lives of more than 10,000 survivors who were enslaved, exploited, or at risk.

O.U.R. has calculated that it takes $1,200 to liberate one child from the human trafficking ring. With your help, we can all finally end the inhumane practice of child sex trafficking that suppresses the voices of hundreds of thousands of people who roam in the shadows of society cold, hungry, and powerless. You can help answer the prayers of tens of thousands of children who seek to live a promising life by committing yourself to this noble cause.

It is a wonderful organization that I financially support with my allowance, and I highly recommend you look into it as well.

———

A MANTRA THAT I frequently chant to myself when I face an almost insurmountable challenge is: "Failure is not an option, for with God nothing shall be impossible."

Together, we must liberate those who do not have a voice. Failure, in this situation, is simply not an option. It is up to us to create a more thoughtful, caring, and peaceful world for generations to come; to leave behind a society that was greater than the one we inherited.

For more information about Tim Ballard and his work, please visit:

Operation Underground Railroad (O.U.R.)
1950 W. Corporate Way
Anaheim, CA 92801
www.OurRescue.org
+1 (818) 850-6146
EIN: 46-3614979

For those who have swiftly taken interest in the O.U.R. organization, I sincerely thank you for joining the good fight.

CHAPTER 14

Final Thoughts

BEFORE I REACH my final conclusion, I would like to sincerely thank you for devoting your time and mental energy to reading this book. My purpose here was not to convince you to believe one way or another; instead, I simply wanted you to *think*.

I want you to question your entire political belief system, not just today, but every day. As new facts emerge, I want you to reassess your stance on certain issues. I encourage you to read books that contradict your current political ideology and explore different news sources, as this is the only way we will grow as a society.

I started writing this book at the age of thirteen, and finished it two months shy of my fifteenth birthday. I joyfully devoted a year and a half of my life to writing every night, after finishing my schoolwork and extracurricular activities, to show the world a new level of thinking that is beyond Democratic or Republican, beyond Left or Right, beyond Progressive or Tea Party. It is a fresh way of thinking that I believe is one possible road map for the survival of our Constitutional Republic.

Am I a conservative liberal? Or perhaps a liberal conservative?

Only time will tell how the media will classify me. But I consider myself a *smart capitalist* who is *pro-human* from conception to grave.

In 2017, I attended the inauguration of President Trump and met Vice President Pence. In 2019, I participated in conference calls with Bernie Sanders. In 2020, I visited the campaign headquarters of Mike Bloomberg and made donations to seven presidential candidates from three different political parties, just to get on their mailing lists.

When I was little, my family nicknamed me "the pint-sized conservative," but in truth, I am a lover of *all politics*. I am a true political strategist who does not fall into traditional camps, at least not at this point in my life.

But I do understand that as a former die-hard conservative who supported lower taxes, a scale-back of government regulations, and a tighter preservation of Judeo-Christian values—the only thing I can say to those who disapprove of my decision to leave my former way of thinking is that it didn't leave me; I left the Republican Party.

After conducting swaths of research, my conscience simply did not allow me to support a party that primarily works in the interests of only a few. Trickle-down economics is a fraudulent ideology that does not benefit the working middle class. In fact, Republicans adhere to an economic philosophy that is counterintuitive to their desires for balanced budgets and a reduction of spending.

The GOP is in favor of the United States spending more money on our military but wants to decrease spending for domestic programs that help the nearly 40 million people who live below the poverty line. Most Republicans claim to be pro-life, yet they refuse to acknowledge that their refusal to raise the minimum wage forces many women to have abortions in order to avoid utter financial collapse. Republicans are not pro-life when they purchase AR-15-style weapons with the capacity to take out nine people within 30 seconds; they are not pro-life when they scoff at the idea of providing comprehensive, universal healthcare that will literally save thousands of people; they are not pro-life when they are in favor of maintaining an antiquated criminal justice system that wrongly sentences innocent people to death.

Republicans are not pro-family when they support a president who implemented an immigration policy that led to children being ripped away from their families and put into cages. They are not pro-family when they are willing to send thousands of young men and women into the battle lines of unnecessary and costly oil wars that rain human carnage.

Republicans, frankly, are mired in political hypocrisy. They claim to be in favor of preserving what made America great while their methods are inherently counterproductive. The politicization of the media has indoctrinated voters to support policies that are not in their best interest. If someone is in favor of a balanced budget, then why not reduce spending for all federal programs, instead of slashing the domestic budget while jacking up defense funds? Conservative voters who are in favor of upholding our Constitution must challenge themselves to vote for candidates who will empower Congress's constitutional duty to declare war.

The Democratic Party, however, needs to address their serious political flaws as well. While Democrats are in favor of imposing tighter gun control laws, support affordable healthcare coverage, and oppose capital punishment, they fail to acknowledge that abortion is a direct result of the disposal of hundreds of thousands of human lives every year. Democrats also engage in histrionically driven identity politics that fosters nothing but hatred, resentment, and discrimination.

The color of someone's skin does not determine their worth. Everyone has the right to practice any religion they take faith in—as well as the right to not believe in a higher power at all. Women deserve one hundred percent, full equal rights to men. Gay couples deserve the right to marry and raise children. Atheists deserve the right to speak their minds. And of course, it is entirely unacceptable for any official to discriminate on external factors such as creed, sexual orientation, or gender.

These principles are wholeheartedly accepted by the majority of American society. But the Democratic Party weaponizing these factors does not contribute to the causes of the disadvantaged; it only detracts from it. Choosing a product or service simply because they employ more of one characteristic over another is inverse discrimination that only degrades the political belief system of progressives, and is why identity politics is repelling a large part of America.

Furthermore, Democratic politicians who use profane language, rip up speeches, and advocate for physical violence against those who have differing opinions, only deter independent voters from casting their ballots for them. The moment six Democrat representatives walked out of the State of the Union Address is when the 2020 election was decided.

America was completely *turned off*.

We need to prove that we can put forth capable leaders who can be trusted with navigating the nation in the right direction. I believe that we need to be bold, but practical; passionate, but not histrionic.

The political landscape is currently in a depression; most conservatives reject racism and bigotry while in favor of the free enterprise system. Many Democrats want progressive change but dislike the identity politics game.

It is time for both Democrats and Republicans to clean up their acts, redefine their messaging, and rebrand their images.

It is time we bridge the gap of common sense between the two parties, and give Independent voters something to believe in.

I plan on writing more books before I graduate from high school, particularly in the areas of elections, criminal justice reform, and my favorite subject of all, Supreme Court Decisions.

I hope that somehow, some way, I will be part of the reshaping of American political thought. I hope that one day I will be fortunate enough to attend a great college, a stellar law school, and find a supportive employer who will help me continue to serve the world.

For I am the new voice of Generation Z.

And we can't wait to show you what the future holds.

AUTHOR MESSAGE

IF YOU ENJOYED reading this book, please share your thoughts on Amazon and Goodreads. **Reviews make or break a book,** and I really want to show my publisher, family, and friends that I have a future in writing political books. Also, please visit my website to learn more about my upcoming projects, signings, and giveaways, and follow me on social media:

WEBSITE: www.JettJamesPruitt.com
FACEBOOK: @presidentpruitt
INSTAGRAM: @jettjamespruitt
TWITTER: @jett_pruitt

Read my latest news articles at:
WWW.THEGENZPOST.COM

Email me at:
EDITOR@THEGENZPOST.COM

Or write me at:
Vanderbilt Publishing, LLC
ATTN: Jett James Pruitt
2000 PGA Blvd, Suite 4440
Palm Beach Gardens, FL 33408

Until Next Time,

Jett J. Pruitt

the ★ ★ ★ ★ ★
GEN Z
post

WWW.THEGENZPOST.COM